COLONISTS
FOR SALE

Other books by
Clifford Lindsey Alderman

RUM, SLAVES AND MOLASSES
The Story of New England's Triangular Trade

THE RHODE ISLAND COLONY

THE ROYAL OPPOSITION
*The Story of the British Generals
in the American Revolution*

Clifford Lindsey Alderman

COLONISTS FOR SALE

THE STORY OF INDENTURED SERVANTS IN AMERICA

MACMILLAN PUBLISHING CO., INC.
New York

Copyright © 1975 Clifford Lindsey Alderman. All rights reserved. No part of this book may be reproduced or transmitted in any form or by any means, electronic or mechanical, including photocopying, recording or by any information storage and retrieval system, without permission in writing from the Publisher. Macmillan Publishing Co., Inc., 866 Third Avenue, New York, N.Y. 10022. Collier-Macmillan Canada Ltd. Printed in the United States of America

1 2 3 4 5 6 7 8 9 10

Library of Congress Cataloging in Publication Data
Alderman, Clifford Lindsey. Colonists for sale: the story of indentured servants in America.
Bibliography: p.   Includes index.
1. Indentured servants—Juvenile literature. [1. Indentured servants. 2. United States—Social life and customs—Colonial period, ca. 1600–1775] I. Title.
HD4875.U5A66   301.44′93′0973   74–23057
ISBN 0-02-700220-9

CONTENTS

1 · The Frightful Journey   1

2 · How It Began   11

3 · Spirits and Newlanders   28

4 · Servant-Snatching in Ireland
    and Scotland   42

5 · White Slaves in Virginia   53

6 · How They Fared
    in Maryland   66

7 · Land of Promise,
    Often Broken   78

8 · Servants in the
    Southernmost Colonies   91

9 · New York, the Palatine Fiasco
    and New Jersey   107

10 · How New England
     Handled the Servants   127

v

CONTENTS

11 · The Soldiers
and Peter Francisco   140

12 · Others Who Made Good   153

13 · A Summing Up   172

For Further Reading   176

Bibliography   177

Index   181

COLONISTS
FOR SALE

1

THE FRIGHTFUL JOURNEY

In 1750 a congregation of German immigrants in the colony of Pennsylvania scraped together enough money to buy what they had greatly desired for their church in the settlement of New Providence—an organ. Not many churches in the American colonies had organs by the middle of the eighteenth century and there were few if any American organ makers then. Importation of the instruments from Europe was the rule. Because of this and perhaps also because the settlers of New Providence put more trust in an organ made in Germany, they ordered it from there. They commissioned an organist, Gottfried Mittelberger, from the duchy of Württemberg in southern Germany, their homeland, to arrange for the shipping and to escort the precious instrument to America himself.

Mittelberger left his village of Enzweihingen and traveled a short distance to Heilbronn in the duchy of Baden, where the organ was. Heilbronn is on the Neckar River, which flows northwestward through

1

Heidelberg and into the Rhine River. After oversee-
ing the packing and loading of the organ into a riv-
erboat, Mittelberger boarded the craft and began
the long journey down the Rhine to Rotterdam,
Holland's greatest seaport. His experiences on the
voyage and during his stay in Pennsylvania prompted
him to write an account of them later.

Jammed into the boat with him were a large
number of people from southern Germany and the
German-speaking part of Switzerland who were also
bound for Pennsylvania. Most of them were farmers
and their families, although there were some artisans, mostly mechanics, and a few scholars and other
educated people. All had one thing in common—
they were simple, trustful folk who had been told of
the glories of the promised land of Pennsylvania, its
beauty, fertility, freedoms and the great opportunities that lay ahead of them to improve their way of
life. They were looking forward to their arrival in
Philadelphia with the keenest anticipation, for their
lives in Germany and Switzerland had not been easy.
They had saved enough money to pay their passage
to Rotterdam and across the Atlantic—or so they
thought and had been told.

The unexpected and shocking frightfulness of
their venture began with the passage to Rotterdam.
There were thirty-six customhouses along the way,
one for each of the little duchies and principalities
through which they passed. Again and again the riv-

erboat had to stop for an examination of the cargo and the payment of customs duties or tolls imposed for passage through the region. It took such boats four or five, sometimes six, weeks to reach Rotterdam. For Gottfried Mittelberger himself, the entire journey from Enzweihingen to Rotterdam lasted seven weeks. The boat was packed from stem to stern, and the terribly crowded conditions made the river trip a nightmare. But this trip was easy compared to what lay ahead for the passengers.

First came a long delay in Rotterdam while the ship that was to take them to America loaded cargo and waited for late-arriving shipments. Mittelberger did not say just how long they were there, but he wrote that the usual delay for such vessels was five or six weeks. During this time the several hundred passengers had to shift for themselves.

The people had not expected this delay, and since food and other necessities were very high-priced in Rotterdam, they found the money they had brought dribbling away. Some became penniless and others spent almost all they had, with their transatlantic passages still not paid. This made no difference to the promoters of the emigration to America; in fact, they were counting on it.

At last the time for embarking came. The shipping company took no precautions for the safety of the passengers as they crowded aboard, pushing and shoving, each anxious to have the best choice of accommodations. Mittelberger saw a man with two children crossing a slimy, ramshackle gangway into the ship; the children slipped, fell overboard and were drowned.

Mittelberger himself seems to have suffered no privation during the voyage; his passage money was assured and presumably he had a cabin to himself and dined with the officers. But what he observed tore his heart with pity and anguish.

He wrote that the emigrants were packed like herrings into the space set aside for them. Bunks two feet wide and six feet long had been placed side by side. Into each bunk went a passenger and all his belongings, including tools and implements, water barrels and provisions, if he had any left.

The vessel crossed the North Sea and put in at Cowes on the Channel coast of England. There some cargo was discharged and examined, customs duties paid and more cargo loaded for Philadelphia. The ship was in Cowes nine days. Then she began the Atlantic passage. From Rotterdam to Philadelphia the voyage lasted fifteen weeks.

Mittelberger wrote: "The journey is made amid such hardships as no one is able to describe." But he did describe it to the best of his ability, and the account is enough to turn one's stomach.

He wrote of the vile conditions in which the emigrants lived. The rations were scanty, stale and had a sharp smell. Some of the meat was so putrid that a dog would have turned up his nose at it. Warm food was served only three times a week. The water was often black and full of worms.

A foul stench filled the passengers' quarters. Almost all were sick at one time or another. Many were seasick and, unable to reach the upper deck in time, vomited in their bunks. Many suffered from fever, dysentery, constipation, boils and the seafaring man's disease of that time, scurvy. Scurvy results from a lack of green vegetables or such citrus fruits as lemons or limes in the diet, and causes the gums to swell and bleed. Mittelberger called it mouth-rot.

On the stormy Atlantic, when a gale rose, conditions were made worse. As the vessel rolled and pitched, plunging down deep into the troughs between the tremendous seas, people were thrown about helter-skelter. In their terror, they thought the vessel was lost, and they cried and prayed piteously to be saved.

The passengers grew irritable and fights broke out between them. Mittelberger wrote that those who were not ill sometimes came near killing each other in these brawls. And among the people were some who lost no opportunity to rob and cheat others in the hope of improving their impoverished condition.

Mittelberger told of hearing passengers cry: "Oh,

that I was at home again and had to lie in my pigsty!"
"O God, if I only had a piece of good bread or a
fresh drop of water."

Many died. One would think that the promoters
of the emigration would have made some effort to
keep the passengers healthy, since it would have
been to their profit when the vessel arrived at Philadelphia. But they evidently considered it cheaper
to lose a substantial part of the human cargo and to
deliver others in poor physical condition than to
spend more to give the people decent quarters, food
and water.

Those who died were heaved overboard without
ceremony. One wretched woman died in childbirth,
unable to deliver the child because of her condition.
Her quarters were far aft, and since the body could
not easily be brought forward and on deck through
the close-packed mass of humanity, it was stuffed
through a porthole and into the sea.

The small children among the passengers suffered
the most. Mittelberger wrote that those between one
and seven years old seldom survived these voyages.
He added that measles and smallpox often broke out
aboard the transports and the younger ones usually
contracted one or the other and died.

Of the older passengers, those who were able to
creep on deck occasionally for a breath of fresh air
sometimes suffered falls in rough weather, as the
ship tossed in mountainous seas, and were crippled.

Others were swept overboard, and Mittelberger made no mention of any effort to save them.

Mittelberger was not a skillful writer, but his diary conveys a vivid image of the passengers' quarters—the fearful smell, the moans of the sick, the cries and pitiful prayers of others, the wailing of children, the disorder, the gauntness of those close to starvation. It must have been a living hell.

As the voyage neared its end, after what must have seemed an eternity, a new catastrophe fell upon the passengers. The food supply had been scanty at best —except that for the officers' table, of course, and doubtless the crew's—but now even that ran short, due to the unusual length of the stormy voyage. The emigrants were fed only ship's biscuit—hardtack— that had long since spoiled and was infested with weevils.

At last, land was sighted. Those who could do so crawled on deck, weeping for joy and thanking God for saving them. Even the very sick began to feel better. All thought that their troubles were over, not knowing that they had only begun. For most of the emigrants, what lay ahead was as bad, in its way, as the torments they had already undergone.

As soon as the ship docked in Philadelphia, the passengers were told that no one whose passage money was not paid or who could not give good security for its payment would be allowed to go ashore. The emigrants had paid at least 40 florins for the trip down the Rhine, as well as exorbitant amounts to provide themselves with food and lodging during the long wait in Rotterdam and additional costs at Cowes. And the passage from Rotterdam to Philadelphia cost 60 florins (£10 in English money, a large sum in those days), except for children between five and ten, who went for half fare, and those under five, who were given free passage. Few could afford to pay such a charge now.

A handful of them had managed to keep enough Dutch florins or German rix-dollars to pay for the voyage or had relatives waiting who would pay the money, so they were allowed to depart. The rest waited for their unknown fate.

Each day thereafter, prosperous English, Dutch and German colonists came from Philadelphia and surrounding towns, some as much as a twenty- to forty-hour ride away, and boarded the ship to bargain for the services of the penniless passengers. Those who suited their buyers signed indentures—bonds which required them to serve their new masters for from three to six years without wages in return for the passage money and food, clothing and lodging during the service. The buyer would then pay the captain or an agent of the shipping company the amount agreed upon for the passage and take his human purchases with him.

All these unfortunate people were to become slaves with white skins—indentured servants who were indeed slaves in every sense of the word until they gained their freedom. Nor did all gain that freedom when their terms of servitude had expired.

Strength was what most buyers wanted. They had little use for scholars, teachers and other educated people, although there was some interest in mechanics. Hands to work in the fields of Pennsylvania were in great demand—most of all, those who could hew down great forest trees, remove stumps and undergrowth and clear land for new fields and meadows. A muscular, healthy young man would get off with three years of servitude, but women, children and older men had to serve six years. Children between five and ten signed indentures, or had them signed for them by their parents, that required them to work without pay until they came of age at twenty-one.

The very sick were sent to hospitals; if they recovered they had to serve long enough to pay for their passage, upkeep and medical costs. Children of such parents or of those unable to work often had to serve additional time to pay off these costs. Families were often separated, not to see each other for years, sometimes never again.

The voyage described by Gottfried Mittelberger was not an unusual one. A great many other emigrations took place under similar wretched and cruel conditions. But the miseries of these transatlantic crossings were only the beginning of the story of indentured servitude in America, which was a well-established system in the seventeenth and eighteenth centuries.

A sizable number of the settlers in the American colonies during that period came as indentured servants. Many suffered from hard labor under conditions to which they were not accustomed, and some died. Others were harshly treated by the masters who had bought them. Still others served months and sometimes years of extra servitude, cheated by unscrupulous masters of the freedom they should have gained when their terms of servitude expired. On the whole, the story of this system is not a pleasant one.

2

HOW IT BEGAN

During the terrible summer of 1607 more than half of the slightly over a hundred all-male settlers of the first permanent American colony at Jamestown, Virginia, died of dysentery and malaria. When the following winter ended, only thirty-eight of the men remained alive, in spite of the heroic achievement of Captain John Smith in trading for food with the Indians. But with the arrival of ships from England in the spring with food and new colonists, Virginia began to expand and thrive.

To the north, when the Pilgrims settled Plymouth, the story was much the same. Half of the colonists died in the winter of 1620–21. Nevertheless, the survivors planted crops and worked them, so after a good summer they were able to enjoy a plentiful first Thanksgiving. And as in Virginia, the Plymouth colony prospered and grew in size. Farther north, stern Puritans settled Boston in 1630, and the colony grew and spread out into surrounding settlements rapidly.

Other settlements in America soon followed. A tide of immigration, at first chiefly from England, set in. In the early years of colonization, although many "gentleman" settlers brought servants with them, most of the work of establishment and making a living was done by the settlers themselves—men, women and children.

This soon changed. As farms and plantations grew larger and trade increased, so did the need for more labor increase. In Maryland and Virginia especially, once it was discovered that fortunes could be made from large tobacco plantations, the need for hands to work in the fields became acute. This need was greatest in the colonies from New York south; for some time New England was largely a region of small farms and, on the seacoast, fishermen. Soon, in the colonies where sea trade grew important, there was a demand for clerks in merchants' counting-houses, coopers and cargo handlers on the wharves, ropemakers and sailmakers, carpenters to put up new houses, warehouses and other buildings, many other artisans, and servants for the houses of prosperous men. However, New England used fewer indentured servants than some other colonies that had good seaports. New England was more inclined to use the labor of freemen, especially boys who were apprenticed to work without wages in order to learn a trade.

In brief, there were shortages of all kinds of labor. True, new settlers were arriving from England as well as other parts of Europe. But not enough working people wanted to or were financially able to give up their homes abroad and take the risks of coming to a new land. Yet England, Germany, Switzerland, Ireland, Scotland and other countries were veritable gold mines for this labor so precious to the new colonies.

Look first at England. For centuries the common people there lived under a feudal system that had been introduced by William the Conqueror after he subdued the country in 1066. They were little better than slaves to the great lords who owned vast lands and big manor houses.

Many English peasants lived on lands owned by the monasteries and abbeys of the English church, which were mostly enormously rich and as tyrannical toward their tenant farmers as the great lords. In the sixteenth century King Henry VIII severed ties between the English church and Rome when the pope refused to grant him a divorce from Catherine of Aragon so that he could marry Anne Boleyn. The highest-ranking bishop in England, the Archbishop of Canterbury, then granted the divorce. With that, Henry began the dissolution of the monasteries and abbeys. This had little beneficial effect on the peasants who lived on church lands, since Henry sold or gave away most of the properties to the lords. The farmers continued to live in want and misery.

Soldiers formed another poverty-stricken group. Under the feudal system England had no regular army. The great lords maintained their own forces; in case of war these soldiers could be called in to fight for the king. Feudalism waned slowly in England, but by the time of Henry VIII's reign it had almost vanished and the lords, unable to keep up their little private armies, had turned them out.

Under Henry's daughter, the great Queen Elizabeth I, science had begun to make tremendous strides. Machinery and new types of tools were developed during her reign, from 1558 to 1603, that could do a man's work or help him do it more quickly, so fewer workmen were needed in many trades. The powerful system of guilds, much like modern trade unions, grew weaker as machines forced many workers out of their jobs.

By the time the feudal system was officially abolished, during the reign of King Charles II in the seventeenth century, the transition from feudalism to a commercial economy had already taken place and a further change to an industrial one was in progress.

Perhaps the worst economic disaster fell upon the thousands of tenant farmers who lived on the lords' lands. Most agricultural villages had had areas called "common land" where all the local peasants could graze their cattle. Now individuals were allotted small farms and the common lands were enclosed by hedges so that the lords could use them for grazing large flocks of sheep. Raising sheep for wool to be manufactured into woolen cloth had become a highly important and profitable business for England. The small farmers could not afford to buy large flocks of sheep or enclose them on their own small acres. Furthermore, with the common lands enclosed, they could no longer graze the cattle upon which they depended largely for a living. Many could not exist on their small farms and became wanderers searching for work. The enclosure system, which began in the sixteenth century but increased sharply at the beginning of the eighteenth, was bitterly opposed and hated by the common people, yet it continued to spread rapidly nonetheless.

All these deprivations combined to create a great mass of poverty-stricken people. The tendency was for them to drift to the large cities where industry offered at least some chance to find work. But because most were unskilled at any trade, there was little or no work for them. Many became beggars or turned to crime, even though a person could be hanged for a petty offense such as stealing a loaf of bread.

Their misery was so great that whenever they obtained a little money they spent it not on food but on gin, which was cheap then and could provide some solace from their troubles. The slum districts of London and other large cities became cesspools filled with drunkards, dissolute women, thieves, pickpockets, beggars and other rogues, as well as diseased persons. Those who could pay for lodgings lived in filthy, ramshackle rookeries; those who could not, found their only homes in the streets and alleys.

Conditions grew worse as the seventeenth century wore on. By 1688 poverty was so widespread that an English economist calculated that the incomes of more than half the country's population were less than their living expenses. He estimated that there were 849,000 families of this kind, averaging 3¼ persons per family. The English poor laws provided for the collection of taxes for the relief of the needy. Yet in 1685 poor law taxes collected were only £665,000. This would have been about $3.75 a year per family in United States currency at its original value of about $5.00 per British pound sterling. Even at that time, when this amount would buy far more than today, it was a pitifully inadequate sum.

In the English cities paupers jammed the workhouses, which were practically prisons where penniless people were put to work at whatever could be found for them to do. Controlled by brutal overseers, they subsisted on food that was scanty, of poor quality and often rotten.

The actual prisons were usually very overcrowded, even though in London carts filled with condemned convicts rumbled almost daily to the public gallows called Tyburn Tree, where mobs pushed and jostled to get a better view of the hangings. But these and executions in other cities could not begin to reduce the surplus of felons in England.

Something had to be done to get rid of the unwanted poor and criminals. The law allowed convicts to be transported out of England, and many were sent to the West Indies and the American colonies. But this made no more than a dent in the overpopulation, and convict labor was unpopular in the colonies because most felons were of the lowest character, poor workers who made trouble.

The English government finally decided that the best possible solution was to persuade the more deserving poor to emigrate to America. The government's idea was excellent, but carrying it out was quite another thing. In spite of their wretchedness, the poor were not at all anxious to go to America.

For one thing, it was unknown territory and therefore frightening. For another, many realized that emigration to America would mean hard work in the wilderness across the ocean, and they preferred to live in poverty without exerting themselves. If the English government was to succeed in dumping its unwanted surplus poor in America, it was either going to have to find ways of making emigration attractive or use forcible means.

England was not the only source to satisfy the American colonies' need for labor. In parts of Germany and the German-speaking region of Switzerland there were plenty of people who might be persuaded to leave if they could be made to see America as a land of opportunity.

The Rhine, one of the great rivers of the world, also has some of the finest scenery in Europe. Flowing northward, it traverses, between Mainz and the vicinity of Bonn, what is known as the Rhine gorge for a distance of about eighty miles. On both sides of the majestic, swift-flowing river, as well as the several smaller tributaries that empty into it there, hills and mountains rise. Capping their summits are dozens of ancient castles, today mostly in various stages of ruin, about which strange and romantic legends have grown.

Below the castles, terraced vineyards ramble down the hillsides to towns and villages huddled between the river and the heights. It is rich agricultural country, famed for its fine wines. A good place to live and prosper, one would think.

The Germans of the Rhine country did love their homeland and would have prospered in the seventeenth century but for the hardships they suffered in those years. At that time the Rhineland, including what was then a collection of little principalities, duchies and counties called the Lower Palatinate, was the trampling ground of armies that marched across it. On their way they seized and destroyed castles, burned villages, looted and committed terrible atrocities among the inhabitants.

These troubles began with the Thirty Years War from 1618 to 1648, involving Germany, Austria, Spain and France. In 1620 the Rhine region was overrun by troops from the Netherlands, which was then held by Spain. There followed a period of peace, but late in the seventeenth century Louis XIV of France decided to conquer the Spanish Netherlands, and raised a huge army to do it. The army's route, in this conflict known as the Dutch War, lay through the Rhineland. In 1688 French soldiers fell upon the medieval walled town of Andernach and burned it. Another French army wrought much more fearful devastation in 1689.

The aftermath of the Dutch War was less frightful, but it brought new hardships to the hard-working peasants of the Rhineland. All the little states that formed the region were governed by petty princes, many of whom occupied the famed castles of the region. When Louis XIV built his enormous palace at Versailles just outside Paris, the rulers of the Rhineland states were envious of its splendor and luxury. They tried to imitate, on a small scale, the way of life that the French king had established.

The bill for their efforts, of course, was paid by

the peasants. Cruel taxes were levied on the farmers, and the long succession of toll stations on the Rhine made the cost of shipping wines and other products to Rotterdam for export so high that little profit remained to them.

Thus the common people of the Palatinate went from the suffering and destruction the wars had brought, to lives of poverty in which they could barely scrape out an existence. They were ripe for a change. Many were ready to move to any place that would give them a chance for better lives.

In the German-speaking part of Switzerland that rims southern Germany, the land had been torn by religious strife and the rule of petty tyrants. Towering Alpine peaks limited agriculture largely to dairy farming. The discontented peasants there were also ready for a change.

Ireland, the beautiful Emerald Isle, had its thousands of poor, miserable people, too. For centuries the country had suffered the persecutions and discriminations of its overlord, England. The harsh Protector, Oliver Cromwell, vented upon Ireland his Puritan hatred of Catholics when he landed an army in Dublin in 1649. For the next three years he devastated Ireland, capturing town after town, butchering not only the Irish soldiers, but also innocent men, women and children by the thousands. Five-sixths of the Irish population died, while most of those who remained were pushed into the infertile land of western Ireland. On the better land, Englishmen established great estates.

In 1660, when the Irish people had managed to make some recovery and established an export trade in woolens, the English Parliament forbade this encroachment upon England's own trade in woolen cloth. When the Irish turned to exporting raw wool, this trade, too, was stopped. Meanwhile, Irish tenant farmers who rented land on the big English-owned estates were forced to pay such high rents that eviction of tenants who were behind in their payments was a common sight. Many could find no other living and starved.

Here were people who needed no persuasion to emigrate from Ireland; they simply wanted to learn where they could find a new homeland that offered some chance to live decently, and how they might get there.

In Scotland, conditions for tenant farmers in the Highlands were also bad, especially in the eighteenth century when several poor crop years added to their poverty as grasping landlords kept raising their rents. Yet in spite of the money-squeezing landowners, some of these Scots had somehow scraped together over the years enough money to pay their way to America. They, too, only needed to find out what the colonies offered.

Thus, on the one hand, most of the American colonies were crying out for new settlers to provide labor and skills; on the other, English, Germans, Swiss, Irish and Scots had reasons to seek new homes, but to them America was a wilderness that did not seem to warrant the expense of the long voyage across the stormy Atlantic. How could they be convinced that the colonies were, instead, a promised land?

The first to realize how this might be accomplished was the Virginia Company (also called the London Company), an organization of merchants and wealthy men in England chartered by King James I to establish the first permanent American colony of Virginia. The English government, in financial trouble and at its wits' end about how to solve the problem of its great masses of poor, was only too glad to let a private company try it.

The settlement at Jamestown, Virginia, in 1607, had been made by a group of "gentleman" adventurers more interested in getting what they could out of Virginia than in colonization. But the Virginia Company soon decided that the new settlement offered prospects for long-term profits through actual colonization.

In 1609 it published a broadside, a kind of advertisement, that was circulated in London. All "workmen of whatever craft they may be, blacksmiths, carpenters, coopers, shipwrights, turners and such as know how to plant vineyards . . . and all others, men as well as women, who have any occupation . . ."

were invited to meet at Sir Thomas Smith's house, where they would be enrolled.

The broadside made lavish promises of what those who signed up would receive. Each person was to be given 500 reals. This Spanish silver coin (all kinds of money, especially Spanish, circulated in England then) varied in value over the years, but in American money the amount would have been somewhere between about $25 and $50, a considerable sum in those days. The new colonists were also to be provided with houses, orchards and vegetable gardens, food and clothing, all free from the Virginia company. Moreover, after seven years the settlers would share in the profits the company had made in its venture in Virginia and receive free land. A few years later, Governor Sir George Yeardley promised that the share would amount to as much as a hundred acres apiece.

According to the plan, the new colonists would not be indentured servants since they did not have to sign bonds for any specific length of time, although they would have to remain seven years to share in the profits and land.

It was not long, however, before indentures made their appearance. The first one that is known is dated September 7, 1619, issued by four English gentlemen who proposed to establish what became known as Berkeley Hundred in Virginia. For Berkeley Hundred there were no glittering promises like those of the Virginia Company. The prospective settlers simply signed indentures agreeing to serve a certain length of time to pay off the costs of their transportation to America.

From then on, all settlers who could not pay the cost of their transportation signed indentures. They were no longer freemen, but slaves of the planters who bought them until they worked off their debt. By 1636 forms were printed with blank spaces to be filled in by the prospective settlers and whoever arranged for their transportation.

In England the plan worked only fairly well. In spite of promises and glowing descriptions in the broadsides of the wonders and opportunities that lay ahead of them in the New World, the English common people did not emigrate to America in vast numbers to become indentured servants.

Meanwhile, in America the demand for labor was increasing at a rate that far outdistanced the number of immigrants from Europe. In Maryland and Virginia raising tobacco had become so profitable that the planters were desperate for help to clear the land of its forests and undergrowth and establish larger plantations. In the other colonies the demand was less, but still strong.

In Germany and German-speaking Switzerland there was a large supply of the labor needed for America, but because the dissatisfied people of these regions knew little of the opportunities the New World offered, there was little more than a trickle of emigration until one of America's most famous men, William Penn, solved the problem.

Penn's American colony of Pennsylvania was among the last of the thirteen to be established. In 1682 Penn and some of his followers came to join an advance party which had arrived in 1681 and was already at work surveying and clearing land, laying out Philadelphia. Penn stayed a year to supervise the work and to draw up a set of laws which he was determined should make Pennsylvania free, well governed and prosperous, in order that it should live up to the name of its first settlement, Philadelphia, the City of Brotherly Love. Then he went back to England.

William Penn may be called America's greatest promoter or, as he would be described today, land developer, of his time. Like the Virginia Company and some others in England, he, too, issued a broadside describing the beauty and fertility of Pennsylvania and the opportunities it offered settlers for a good life, freedom and fortune. His description was alluring, and he had it printed in English, German and Dutch. His agents in Europe saw to it that the pamphlets were widely distributed.

Penn's plan was to persuade well-to-do Europeans to emigrate to America, bringing indentured servants with them. Each servant was to be given fifty acres of land as soon as he had paid off the cost of his journey.

The broadside obtained the greatest immediate response in the Palatinate, including the Rhineland, and German-speaking Switzerland as well. Thousands of peasants eagerly seized the chance for relief from the disasters and grinding poverty they had suffered.

Penn had no idea that he was sowing the seeds that would produce the misery described by Gottfried Mittelberger. In fact, most of those who came from Germany and Switzerland were redemptioners, a special class of emigrants who expected to be freemen in America, although few were until they had paid off the unexpected extra cost of the voyage.

Redemptioners signed no indentures before leaving their homelands. They had enough money to pay at least part of their passage to America. Usually they were confident that they could find relatives or friends already in America who would lend or give them the money to settle the unpaid part of the bill. What actually happened to many of the redemptioners aboard Gottfried Mittelberger's ship is a clue to the fate of others whose hopes of paying off their indebtedness upon arrival in America often were disappointed.

The Scottish Highlands also responded quickly to Penn's advertisement. Many Scots emigrated to

America like the Germans and Swiss, as redemptioners.

In Ireland, William Penn's broadsides appealed strongly to the thousands of starving, homeless men who wandered about the island in search of work of any sort. Ships began sailing from Dublin and Cork for a number of American colonies, loaded to the gunwales with hopeful Irish indentured servants.

The demand for indentured servants in America was so great that the colonies which desperately needed labor continued to take them for many years, through the eighteenth century and even into the early nineteenth. Shipping emigrants to America became a big business in England, Germany, Switzerland, Ireland and Scotland. Just how big and how evil a trade it became remains to be seen.

3

SPIRITS AND NEWLANDERS

When the lavish descriptions and promises of the Virginia Company and the broadsides published by William Penn and others failed to attract many of England's vast horde of poor people, the British government looked for another solution to the difficulty. It was provided not by the government but by merchants, shipowners and wealthy men who saw a chance to reap a golden harvest from the trade in indentured servants.

London had the largest share of the English emigrant trade. In the seventeenth century, though far smaller than today, the city was nevertheless vast and sprawling for its time. By 1660 its population was 460,000; by 1700 it had grown to half a million. In 1666 the Great Fire had destroyed much of the city, but it was quickly rebuilt and the expansion of its industry and commerce continued.

Its people included the rich (nobility and successful merchants and manufacturers), the small tradesmen and artisans who were modestly well off and the huge mass of the poor. It had great houses, less pretentious but comfortable brick buildings and hovels in the slums.

One often might see the glittering coach of a nobleman, emblazoned with the insignia of his title and drawn by sleek, prancing horses, rolling through the better streets with footmen in white running in front of it. In London's black fogs, when the city could become as dark as midnight at noon, hackney coaches patronized by those who could afford them groped their way along, guided ahead by a link boy carrying a flaring torch.

On clear days the city's magnificence could be seen, capped by St. Paul's Cathedral on its hill that dominated the city, the royal palaces and the town houses of the rich. Spanning the swift-flowing Thames was London Bridge, solidly lined on both sides with houses and shops whose overhanging upper stories made the narrow roadway look like a tunnel, with a gruesome display of the heads of executed criminals stuck on tall spikes at one end. And there was the splendor of broad Cheapside, the city's central thoroughfare, with its fine shops of goldsmiths, linen drapers and milliners, and excellent taverns.

In contrast, one had only to go into the narrow lanes and alleys of the slums to find incredible wretchedness. As on London Bridge, the overhanging upper stories of the ramshackle houses made these passageways dark and airless. There was no such thing as garbage collection; people simply threw refuse into the gutter until a heavy rain carried at least some of it away. Part of these rotting masses was also disposed of by the great brown rats that scurried about and the croaking ravens that flapped down out of the sky. Often great heaps of garbage and trash blocked big, lumbering wagons and other traffic. The interiors of the buildings were dark, cheerless, verminous, damp and, in winter, cold.

Here lived London's poor, except for those who were in workhouses, hospitals or prisons. Here, in spite of its squalor and filth, was the gold mine that could yield riches to those who sought new colonists for America. But the poverty-stricken and the idlers of the slums did not want to go to America; they were used to their lives in London and wanted to stay there.

Merchants and other agents for American planters, in London and several other large English cities, were greatly disappointed that the broadsides and other advertisements had not worked too well. They decided that if the people could not be influenced in this way, they might be persuaded in some other.

They engaged certain persons to round up, in one way or another, cargoes of colonists for America. These subagents were of every sort—yeomen who owned their own small farms, tradesmen, even doctors who might advise their patients that the excellent climate of America would improve their health. The mayor of the seaport city of Bristol was suspected of having a part in recruiting colonists, and royal palace gossip had it that certain of the queen's titled ladies-in-waiting, in return for money to buy extra clothes and jewels, were not above persuading palace servants to leave for America.

Most of these subagents, however, were men with nothing better to do, and many were downright rogues. These recruiters became known in England as "spirits." Some spirits were slick-tongued individuals who persuaded their prospects with glowing descriptions of the beauty, easy life and opportunities in the colonies, although few had ever been to America.

There were certain places in London where they congregated to ply their trade. One location was the middle aisle of St. Paul's Cathedral. Strange as it may seem, in the seventeenth century this part of the largest and most important church in London became a kind of business street on weekdays. Porters and messengers took short cuts through the aisle. Money lenders and marriage brokers made their headquarters there. Horse traders and people with houses to sell hung out in St. Paul's. Scribes set up their tables to provide letters for those who could not write. Sea captains out of a berth aboard a ship lounged there, hoping to strike up a conversation with some young idler with money who would exchange a good dinner over a bottle for the spinning of some sea yarns. Hawkers, much like the city sidewalk merchants of today, laid out their wares on the tombstones of prominent Englishmen buried in the crypt under the floor. Visitors who were wise kept a close eye on their purses and watches, for the place was overrun with thieves and pickpockets.

St. Paul's swarmed with beggars, too—"rufflers" who claimed to be destitute former soldiers wounded while fighting for their country; "palliards" who used children to gain sympathy; "dommerers" who pretended to be dumb; and "quire birds" (today's expression is "stool pigeons") who had turned king's evidence and testified against their confederates to save their own skins. And also in St. Paul's, the sharp-eyed spirits waited, ready to swoop down on likely prospects.

Another place of business for the spirits was the Royal Exchange in the heart of the City, London's business and financial center. It was a U-shaped building, opening at the front into a large courtyard. Edging this were porticoes over which, on the second floor, were balconies with all sorts of little shops. As at St. Paul's, characters of all kinds milled about the courtyard, among them the hopeful spirits.

As soon as a spirit convinced his prey to go to America, the prospective colonist signed an indenture and was taken to safekeeping until he could be loaded aboard a ship.

Many of the spirits haunted the London slums and those of Bristol and other seaports. It was not difficult to find hungry and thirsty victims who, over a dinner and much liquor, would sign anything put before them. The spirit would then hustle his prey to his headquarters to be added to a waiting company of others, safely kept where they could not escape until a ship was ready for them. An easier way was to pick up a sleeping drunk from the gutter and put him aboard a vessel for America, where, with no indenture, he could be sold to his own disadvantage and the American planter's gain.

Children were valuable and could be enticed with candy to come along with a spirit. Sometimes they, and older people, too, were seized by force. There was not as much of this kidnaping as was generally believed, although it did exist and the people of London became greatly incensed over it. All that was necessary to start a riot in a crowd was to point out some person as a spirit and he would instantly be set upon by angry citizens.

"Cooks' houses" were as popular in London as hot dog and similar stands are today on street corners in New York and other large cities. The cooks' houses specialized in beef and pork pies. Men stationed outside them cried, "Hot! Hot! Get them hot!"

A good many cooks' houses were located in dis-
reputable neighborhoods such as St. Katherine's,
near the Thames and the Tower of London and convenient to the wharves. Since these meat pies were
cheap, the spirits often located their headquarters
near a cook's house and sent food in to the future
emigrants so that none would attempt to escape before they could be shipped out.

Ned Ward, a writer in the early eighteenth century who roved London and wrote some descriptions
of the city's worst aspects, described a visit to a spirit's place of business:

We peer'd in at a Gateway, where we saw Three or
Four Blades [the spirits] well drest with Hawks Coun-
tenances attended with half a Dozen Ragamuffinly Fel-
lows showing Poverty in their Rags and Despair in their
Faces, mixt with a parcel of Wild Young Striplings like
Run-Away Prentices [apprentices] . . . that House, says
my friend, which they are entring is an Office where
Servants for the Plantations bind themselves.

Another description by a writer who called himself the English Rogue told of his falling in with a
spirit who took him to Wapping, also a mean and
shabby section near the wharves. He said he was
taken into a narrow room where spirits sat smoking
pipes so vigorously that for a time he could see nothing but smoke. At last he made out two other men in
the same plight he was, but their conversation was

only about "the pleasantness of the soil of that Continent that they were designed for . . . to the temptation of the air, the plenty of fowl and fish of all sorts; the little labour that is performed or expected having so little trouble in it, that the earth may be accounted a pastime rather than anything of punishment." The English Rogue also told of seeing a number of women in the place, used as bait by the spirits to snare their prey. It was said in 1649 that anyone could obtain a servant for America at one of these places by paying £3 to cover the spirit's fee and the cost of feeding his victims.

Public outcry against the spirits became so loud that the government was forced to take action against their wrongful activities. Bristol, being an important seaport, was the first to pass a law in 1634 requiring that all servants shipped out must be registered, giving their destination and the date their indentures were signed. Those disobeying were to be fined £20. London followed later, although there was already an act of Parliament charging authorities to be alert against kidnaping for the indentured servant trade and to search vessels in the Thames and the Downs at the river's mouth. The new law also required registry but was not well enforced, perhaps because the government was so anxious to be rid of its surplus of poor and idlers.

One spirit operated his business on such a large scale that he was able to offer a great bargain to mer-

chants who wanted servants for America. He was
finally caught when another spirit was convicted of
illegal shipment of indentured servants, turned
king's evidence and told the story of the one who did
business at such low prices. The man, he said, had
been in the trade at St. Katherine's for twelve years.
He would pay anyone who turned a victim over to
him 25 shillings and then sell his captive to a merchant for 40 shillings. He made money because he
exported five hundred servants a year on the average; in one banner year he had shipped out 840 of
them.

Since most spirits were unsavory men with no
principles, some took advantage of the law against
illegal procurement of indentured servants. A group
of them would kidnap a victim and get him aboard a
ship. Then one of the gang would represent himself
as an authorized searcher, "discover" the kidnaped
person, charge the captain with the crime and demand money for keeping his mouth shut. The same
game was used against merchants who shipped out
indentured servants. One who refused to pay the
blackmail found himself in terrible Newgate Prison
charged with kidnaping. This dodge became so
common in the 1670s and 1680s that many honest
merchants were afraid to buy the indenture of any
servant offered by a spirit lest they be accused of
kidnaping.

In Germany and Switzerland the counterpart of

the English spirit was usually called a "newlander"; another less common name for him was "soul-vendor." Most newlanders were well-dressed, prosperous-looking men with big gold watch chains that impressed the simple peasants tremendously. A good many had actually been to Pennsylvania and others pretended they had. All told tall stories of the glories of that colony and how easy it was to make a comfortable fortune there.

The newlanders plied their trade by first making agreements with shipping companies in Rotterdam under which they would be paid in Dutch florins, ducats or Spanish doubloons for the emigrants they delivered to the seaport. There the newlanders would get the emigrants to sign indentures unless they were traveling as redemptioners.

The newlanders were no more scrupulous than the spirits. If German or Swiss peasants already had relatives in America, the newlander might find out about it before he talked with them. Then he might tell these credulous people that he had learned in Philadelphia of the death of one of these relatives, that an inheritance was awaiting them, and that he had the legal power to obtain the money for them as soon as they reached Philadelphia aboard a ship with him. Unfortunately the newlander was rarely a passenger, nor was there any inheritance.

The newlanders knew perfectly well that the great need in Pennsylvania was for laborers and mechanics. Yet almost any healthy person could be sold in Philadelphia and put to work at hard labor on the plantations. The newlanders also went after learned and highly skilled people, even the nobility. More than one impoverished nobleman found himself in Pennsylvania working as a laborer.

One especially shameful trick was to get emigrants to entrust their money to newlanders during the trip down the Rhine to Rotterdam. It would be safe with him from thieves or accidental loss, the newlander would say, not only on the Rhine journey, but during the voyage across the Atlantic, since of course he would be aboard to see that his passengers were well taken care of. Once the ship sailed from Rotterdam, the emigrants never saw him or their money again.

A titled lady fell prey to just such a scheme. She had over a thousand rix-dollars, more than ample to pay the entire cost of the trip for herself, two teen-age daughters and a young son. She was personally acquainted with the newlander to whom she entrusted the money and had no doubts of his honesty. Needless to say, he was not aboard the ship bound for America and the noble lady and her daughters were sold and put to work at menial labor.

Often a newlander returning from Pennsylvania was entrusted by settlers with letters to their relatives or friends in Germany or Switzerland. In Rotterdam the letters would be opened; if they told the truth about the difficulties and hardships so many indentured servants suffered, the letters would be destroyed or, better still, rewritten to tell the wonders of life in Pennsylvania by expert handwriting forgers who were available in Rotterdam.

The story of Johann Karl Buettner is a good example of how a young man who was afflicted with wanderlust fell victim to newlanders. He was born in the eighteenth century in the German duchy of Saxony. His father was a minister who sent Johann to school, where the young man decided to become a doctor.

He was well on his way to his objective as a doctor's apprentice when he became dissatisfied for some reason and returned home. His father then sent him to Dresden to continue his studies, but suspecting Johann might not go there, he sent the young man's two brothers along on the journey.

They reached Dresden, the two brothers left for home and Johann promptly began a roving tour that took him to Prague in present-day Czechoslovakia and on through Hungary to the Balkan countries. At last his journey ended in Hamburg, Germany, with his money almost gone.

After a look at Hamburg, Johann crossed the Elbe River to the suburb of Altona. There he fell into conversation with some friendly and pleasant, though unknown, companions. He felt even better disposed toward them when they discovered he came from Saxony and announced that was their home too.

The men were sharp newlanders. They invited Johann to breakfast and over a bottle of wine they asked if he would not like to see the far-off East or West Indies. Having learned of his medical studies, they said they would pay his way to Amsterdam and give him a letter of recommendation to the captain of a ship bound for the East Indies who needed a ship's surgeon.

Johann enthusiastically agreed. The newlanders treated him to a fine midday meal and put him aboard a ship for Amsterdam. There were some fifty other young men and women among the passengers, also expecting to go to the Indies.

In Amsterdam Johann and the rest were disappointed to be told that a ship for the East Indies had just sailed (she doubtless existed only in the minds of the newlanders and their confederates in Amsterdam). However, a vessel was about to sail for America from Rotterdam and the group was assured that passage to the wonderful New World would be provided for them.

So Johann Karl Buettner and the others were taken to Rotterdam and put aboard the ship. More will be told later about Johann's trials and hardships after he was sold as an indentured servant in Philadelphia.

In this way, English and Dutch merchants built up their profitable trade in indentured servants. England, Germany and Switzerland furnished a large portion of the labor the American colonies needed so badly, but in other countries this shabby business was also done on a sizable scale.

4

SERVANT-SNATCHING IN
IRELAND AND SCOTLAND

Like the Germans and Swiss, the Irish loved their homeland. But when they could not pay the exorbitant rents English landlords demanded, thousands became beggars, wandering about in misery. Those forced to move to barren parts of western Ireland were unable to raise enough crops to feed themselves. To make matters worse, there came several bad seasons when the potato crop, the people's chief source of food, failed.

Agents of merchants and shipping companies found it easy to convince these desperate people that a land of plenty awaited them if they would just go to America. Many did, only to find more hardships, often enough, as well as hatred and persecution in some American colonies because they were Catholics. But as happened in England, other Irishmen refused to leave their country in spite of their wretchedness. Upon these people the agents also preyed.

The agents in Ireland who rounded up indentured servants for America were not known as spirits, as in England. They had no special nickname, but one authority, writing about the Irish problem after Cromwell's invasion, spoke of them as "English slave dealers," which indeed they were, and added, "Ireland must have exhibited scenes in every point like the slave lands in Africa."

England was just as glad to be rid of the starving Irish as to send her own poor and vagabonds to America. Also, Cromwell's Puritan government despised Catholics and believed that with the emigration of a vast number of Irish to the colonies, Ireland would become a strongly Protestant country. At the same time, the Irish emigrants would help ease the pressing need for labor in America.

At first England tried to make forced emigration from Ireland look like punishment for wrongdoing. In 1653 the English government appointed overseers of the poor in Ireland who were to seize beggars or those out of work and punish them. Irish tempers are often hot, and wretched wanderers who would have been glad to take any job that would have kept them alive rebelled against the overseers. Many were punished by being sent to hard labor on the American plantations or the sugar plantations of the British West Indies.

Great numbers of homeless and starving children also roamed about the country. In many cases their parents had died of starvation or disease; in others, the children had somehow become separated from their fathers and mothers when so many people were brutally forced to move to Ireland's west country. A plan to round these children up and ship them to America was seriously discussed but abandoned. There is little evidence that any young children were sent to the colonies without their parents, but any child of twelve or so was considered an adult, able to work, and a good many of them were shipped out.

One merchant who took advantage of this was David Selleck of Boston, who was in the indentured-servant trade and often made voyages between Virginia and London to obtain labor for the tobacco plantations. In 1653 his petition to the Council of State in England to ship 400 Irish children at least twelve years old to New England and Virginia was granted on condition that all of them be beggars or vagabonds.

Selleck had two ships, the *Goodfellow* of Boston and the *Providence* of London. There are no records concerning the *Goodfellow*, whose name certainly did not fit the trade she was in. It is quite possible that the Puritan authorities in Boston refused to accept a shipload of Irish children into the Massachusetts Bay colony, since Catholics were hated and feared there.

However, the *Providence* did sail with passengers to Rappahannock in Virginia, where the servants were exchanged for a cargo of tobacco. They were not all children. Selleck used agents in Ireland to obtain 550 beggars and vagrants—250 women between twelve and forty-five years old and 300 men between twelve and fifty. How many of these sailed in the *Providence* is not known.

It was not always easy to assemble a large cargo of Irish emigrants at that time. The London merchants John Jeffries and Robert Lewellin, who were notorious for obtaining indentured servants illegally, decided on a venture in the Irish trade. They arranged to ship 200 Irish from Dublin to Virginia in 1654, but their agents in the Irish capital had poor luck in getting them. When the ship arrived in Dublin, only thirteen or fourteen persons were waiting and all had been taken from Irish prisons. According to the evidence, the two merchants then got a Dublin agent to organize a gang of ruffians who roved the streets seizing likely looking laborers and hustling them aboard the ship.

English merchants often paid no attention to the rules and regulations of the English Council of State, once they had obtained a license for a voyage. Many Irish emigrants were given no indentures before they sailed, so the vessel's captain could sell them to planters for a longer term of service than indentures issued in Ireland would have allowed.

In Ireland kidnaping did take place, as the records show. Of those instances well supported by evidence, one is reminiscent of the fairy tales in which there is a wicked stepmother or close relative. In this case it was a wicked uncle, and the story is a sad one.

James Annersley was the son and heir of the Earl of Anglesey, Lord Altham. James's father and mother died while he was still a small boy and he went to Dublin to live with his uncle, presumably his guardian until James became of age and would inherit his father's title and estate. Since the uncle was next in line to inherit after James and was an unscrupulous man, he determined to get rid of the boy and seize the title and property for himself.

The uncle arranged to have James Annersley kidnaped and shipped to America in about 1728. The vessel put in at Philadelphia, where the boy was sold as an indentured servant. In vain James tried to convince the authorities he was of noble lineage and had been sent to Pennsylvania unlawfully. They decided he had made up the story to avoid servitude.

The man who bought him lived about forty miles from Philadelphia in the fertile Pennsylvania Dutch country. Whether his master treated James kindly is not known, but the boy was so desperate in his resolve to get back to Britain and confront his false uncle that he ran away. Unlike most older and more clever runaways, however, he was caught and his term of servitude extended as a punishment.

James Annersley served twelve years as an indentured servant. Then, miraculously, some men arrived at the plantation who knew the story of the boy's disappearance from Ireland. Their evidence was so strong that James was sent to Philadelphia, where he was befriended by an influential man, Robert Ellis. Ellis was a personal friend of Vice Admiral Edward Vernon, in command of a British fleet then in the West Indies. James appears to have been sent to the islands, from which Admiral Vernon brought him to England.

James's uncle appears to have been enjoying his ill-gotten title and property and he must have been stunned to learn that his nephew was alive, well, in England and ready to fight for his rights. First, James Annersley, the rightful Earl of Anglesey, wrote a book, partly his own story and partly fiction. It aroused tremendous public interest, but since James did not make enough money from it to bring a suit against his uncle, friends swarmed to his aid.

The trial lasted two weeks, with the judge and jury sitting ten hours a day. The uncle tried to show that James was an illegitimate son, but he failed to convince the jury, which brought in a verdict for James in an hour. He still did not get his title and estate, however, for the uncle appealed the case to a higher court.

James's friends could no longer aid him financially. Nearly twenty years passed while he tried frantically to raise money. At last public opinion was again aroused to a point where donations were flooding in. But before he could renew his suit, James Annersley died in 1760, still without his title and estate.

Although the indentured-servant system had waned by the time of the American Revolution, especially because of the growth of black slavery in the southern American colonies, Irish immigration into America continued. By the middle of the nineteenth century, about a million Irish had come to the New World, many in the earlier years as indentured servants; Ireland sent more indentured servants to America than any other English-speaking country.

In the indentured-servant market, however, the Irish were the least favored of all nationalities, because of their Catholicism and because they were reputed to be sickly. (This may even have been true, as a result of their sufferings in Ireland.) The English immigrants were a mixed lot, some good, some poor servants, but the Welsh, Germans, Swiss and Scots were almost universally welcomed, with the Scots perhaps the most favored of all. Many Scots did emigrate and in general they were of good character, hard workers, and brought the highest prices.

In Scotland the compelling reason for emigration to America was poverty. The country had neither a great amount of manufacturing nor agriculture. The situation in the seventeenth and eighteenth centuries, particularly in the Highlands, was very bad and becoming worse because landlords were driving tenants out by raising their rents. Agents had little difficulty in persuading poverty-stricken Scots to emigrate.

One enterprising Aberdeen agent used an unusual method of advertising to fill a ship with indentured servants. James Smith hired a drummer who went through the Aberdeen streets daily from early January until the middle of March, beating away and announcing a forthcoming voyage to America. Smith also employed bagpipers to do the same thing at a fair in Aberdeen. It cost the merchants who had engaged Smith £160, but apparently the servants were obtained and the money was well spent.

As happened in other countries, there were abuses in the collection of indentured servants in Scotland. Joshua Brown of Philadelphia wrote an account of how his Scottish mother was kidnaped as a girl of twelve or fourteen, put aboard a ship and sent to Pennsylvania. There she was sold to a settler who lived south of Philadelphia. She served out her time as an indentured servant, was freed, married and raised a family.

Another Scottish kidnaping story has not only the frustration of James Annersley's adventures, but much hardship and grief as well. While Peter Williamson was a boy, living with his respectable parents outside Aberdeen, he was sent to the city to live

49

with an aunt, apparently so that he could be educated. At the age of eight, while he was playing along the wharves one day, he was seized by two men who took him to a deserted old barn. There, with others in the same plight, Peter remained until they were transferred to a ship bound for America. They spent about a month in the barn and aboard the vessel before she sailed.

In Philadelphia the captain sold his cargo at a price of £16 apiece for seven years' servitude. Since the passengers were held captive before leaving Scotland, it is likely that few, if any, of them signed indentures beforehand and thus the captain probably made a much larger profit by selling them without certificates that specified the term they must serve. Peter was sold alone to one man and he never knew what happened to his companions on the voyage.

But Peter was lucky. His master was a Scot who himself had been kidnaped, shipped to America and sold when he was a boy. Since he had no children of his own, he took a special interest in his servant, treated him with great kindness and saw that he went to school in the winter when there was little farm work to do.

Peter Williamson remained there until he was seventeen, when his master died. In his will he left Peter his freedom, £120 (no small sum in those days), a horse and some clothing. The boy then went on to become prosperous in Pennsylvania. He became a carpenter and, in a small way, a trader. He made a comfortable living, married a well-to-do farmer's daughter and raised a family.

The pioneering spirit was strong in Peter Williamson, as it was in many an American settler. He bought some land in the wild Pennsylvania border country, built a house and moved there with his wife and children. That was the end of his good luck and the beginning of terrible misfortune.

In 1755, when the last of the colonial wars, the French and Indian, broke out, British General Edward Braddock's army was almost wiped out by Indians and French in western Pennsylvania. The Indians then ran wild in that region, attacking remote settlements. They swooped down on Peter Williamson's farm and carried him off as a prisoner.

After two years' captivity, Peter escaped and made his way back to his farm and to heartbreak, for the Indians had murdered all of his family. With this gruesome discovery, Peter had had enough of America. Sadly, he went back to Scotland.

Bent on revenge for his kidnaping, Peter, like James Annersley, wrote a book about his adventures. The magistrates of Aberdeen were enraged. They prosecuted him for writing an untrue book and circulated a report that his story was a lie. They fined him 40 shillings and ordered the objectionable pages in all copies of his book torn out and burned. They also ordered that he sign a "proclamation" to be published in the newspapers admitting he had lied, and banished him from Aberdeen.

Peter Williamson refused to sign the document and there is no evidence that he paid the fine. Instead he published a new edition of his book, including a description of the magistrates' "justice," and sued them for damages. In 1761 he got a judgment for £100, along with the money he had spent for his trial.

He also sued the shipowners who had hired his kidnapers. He won £200 and costs but was not satisfied and brought another suit against the shipowners. However, this time he lost.

These instances of kidnaping are among the few in which there is conclusive evidence. As in England, Germany and Switzerland, most of the indentured servants from Ireland and Scotland emigrated because going to America seemed to be the only way to escape poverty and persecution.

5

WHITE SLAVES IN VIRGINIA

In America the indentured-servant system originated, as already described, in the first of the colonies, Virginia. Even though at the beginning no indentures were signed and the immigrants from England received free passage across the Atlantic, they had to work seven years without pay. The actual indentured-servant system followed soon afterward.

The promises made by the Virginia (or London) Company outdid those of all other promoters of emigration to America. Unfortunately, those who responded to the invitation later found out how hollow the promises were.

When Lord Thomas Delaware (or De La Warr) was appointed governor of Virginia in 1610, he found the colony in wretched, starving condition, with the Jamestown colonists already embarked in a ship to abandon the settlement. Delaware was an excellent administrator; the ships that accompanied him to Virginia were loaded with food and more settlers, and he soon put the colony on the road to survival. But to accomplish this, he imposed discipline and regulations that were the harshest ever encountered in the American colonies. He organized the settlement into a labor force under commanders and overseers in which the so-called servants were little better off than convicts. In the following years his successor, Sir Thomas Dale, made life even more miserable for them.

Dale put the colonists under martial law. They were organized into companies and squads under officers and marched to and from work in the fields and forests. The smallest violation of discipline was punished with ferocious severity. Those charged with idling at their work were put at the hardest labor for from one to three years. For other small offenses they could be made to work in irons for a year or more. Many were whipped with the cruel cat-o'-nine-tails, a whip made of nine strands of rope or leather knotted at the ends.

There were reports that planters hanged, shot or burned serious offenders alive, even breaking them on the wheel, a horrible execution in which the victim had all the bones in his limbs broken by a man with a heavy iron bar and was then left lashed to a wheel to die slowly. However, there is little well-established evidence that the most frightful of these punishments were actually used.

To make their miseries worse, many servants died

of illness because they were unused to the hot summer climate of Virginia's tidewater country, the low-lying eastern region of the colony where most of the tobacco plantations then were. Malaria especially killed large numbers. A few were able to escape by hiding aboard ships bound for England, although this was prohibited.

Samuel Argall, who served as governor from 1617 to 1619, was not much better than Dale. The servants were still supposed to be freemen at that time, but for violation of Argall's regulations one could be sentenced to slavery for three years, while even being absent from church was punished with a year's slavery.

Such rule of people supposed to be free could not go on. Word of conditions in Virginia was bound to get back to England in spite of the authorities' vigilance in seizing and destroying letters that told the truth, and fewer and fewer Englishmen emigrated to Virginia.

Moreover, those who spent the seven years of labor on the plantations discovered that the Virginia Company's attractive promises were not worth much. The agreement had been that each servant who completed his seven years would receive land, probably a hundred acres, that each man's children who were able to work would receive the same amount of land, and that all would share in the Virginia Company's profits. When the first servants' time was up, however, the company allowed them only fifty acres, although it hoped that "future opportunity" would allow it to give at least two hundred acres. As for the company's profits, the colonists discovered that they must buy shares in the company at £12, 10 shillings each or get nothing.

There were violations of the agreements for labor services, too. In the settlement of Charles City Hundred the original colonists had committed themselves to a three-year term of labor. But between nine and ten years went by and they were still not free of their servitude. They demanded full freedom from Governor George Yeardley and he granted it. While freedom had been given some Virginia servants before that, it was rare that one of them found himself much better off when his term had expired, for he had no money with which to establish himself.

Governor Yeardley served from 1616 to 1617 and again from 1619 to 1621. He was a humane man who made a great change in the servants' condition. He instituted a new system with certain freedoms for the servants, including a voice in Virginia's government. He also changed the method of land ownership. Virginia was then composed of eleven boroughs, or plantations. Yeardley set aside tracts of land in each borough for colonists who had earned the right to land of their own and called for an election of two representatives from each borough for an assembly to make laws governing the colony.

After that, emigration from England to Virginia increased rapidly. Agriculture and industry expanded. And around 1624 the servants began to sign formal indentures. The indentured-servant system made it easier to obtain the immigrants so badly needed to raise the tobacco that had become Virginia's chief source of revenue. Now indentures specified that the servant was to be given passage to America in return for his labor over a certain period of time and that he was to be provided with proper food, clothing and lodging during that time. As for whatever reward the indentured servant was to receive at the end of his term in addition to his freedom, many indentures now stated that he would be compensated "according to the custom of the country."

"According to the custom of the country" could be a trap in which many indentured servants were snared. The words meant nothing, since they left it up to the indentured servant's master in America to decide what "freedom dues," as they were called, he would provide. Some masters were generous and would give a freed indentured servant a piece of land, food (usually Indian corn), sometimes tobacco that was as good as money, a complete set of new clothing and some implements that would enable him to start his own little farm, marry, raise a family and perhaps, in time, prosper.

The stingy masters or those dissatisfied with a servant could give nothing at all if they wished. A great many indentured servants found themselves with no better prospect at the end of their terms than living out their lives as hired men on some farm or plantation. Wise emigrants from abroad saw to it that the freedom dues were listed in their indentures before they signed them.

Even worse off, usually, were those who came to America without signing written indentures. The agent in Britain simply made a verbal agreement with the prospective servant, and this, of course, was worth nothing when the man or woman reached America. Such immigrants were often sold for longer terms than if they had signed indentures before leaving, since they were at the mercy of the ship captain or whoever sold them in America, but in time laws were enacted setting limits on the term a man, woman or child should serve.

In the earlier years of the indentured-servant system, large numbers of English paupers, vagabonds, beggars and rogues obtained by the spirits were shipped to Virginia to labor under the blazing sun in the tobacco fields. Immigrants who were skilled in trades were also in demand, and Thomas Jefferson wrote that a freeman who could handle a pen rarely made as much as an artisan in Virginia. Yet the field labor was needed so badly that under the indentured-servant system many a tailor, shoemaker or weaver was forced into the tobacco fields.

A large number of convicts were shipped to Virginia as well, many of them political prisoners. "Uneasy lies the head that wears a crown," wrote Shakespeare, and for centuries it was true in Europe. Conspiracies, big and small, were always festering in England. Noblemen convicted of high treason had the privilege of having their heads chopped off; untitled plotters found guilty were hanged. But many political prisoners languished in prison in the Tower of London when it was suspected but not proved that they were scheming to topple a king or queen from the throne. A convenient way to get rid of them was to ship them to America, usually to slave on a Virginia or Maryland tobacco plantation.

Prisoners of war were also shipped out. In 1650 Cromwell, having subdued Ireland, decided to invade and conquer Scotland. While Cromwell was busy in Scotland, the rightful heir to the British throne, Charles II, seized the opportunity to come out of exile in continental Europe and invade England, supported partly by a Scottish army. But Cromwell, having smashed another such army in Scotland, marched south, met Charles at the battle of Worcester, crushed the invasion, forced Charles to flee back to France and took many Scottish prisoners. He shipped 110 of them to Virginia. They made good workers and, later, free citizens.

In 1685, when Catholic James II was on the throne, his illegitimate son, the Duke of Monmouth, raised a Protestant army in the hope of overthrowing his father and becoming king. John Churchill, ancestor of the famous Winston Churchill, led a royal army against Monmouth's troops and beat them soundly. A number of the rebel prisoners were also sent to Virginia.

Some political prisoners shipped to America were as troublesome to Virginia's English government as they had been in England. In Gloucester County in 1663 a group of them were suspected of plotting a rebellion to regain their freedom. As so often happens, one of the plotters turned traitor and exposed the scheme to the authorities, who put an end to it. The traitor was rewarded with freedom and 5,000 pounds of tobacco, and the indignant planters complained to the government in England against sending any more political prisoners to Virginia. The London government would have liked to continue, but by 1671 it decided to stop. In fact, "Jail Birds," as they were called, of any kind were unpopular in all the colonies. Led by Virginia, the others also began to search incoming ships to seize convicts and send them back to England.

Convicts were hated, but the life of many innocent indentured servants was not a happy one either. Their lodgings, huts or cabins built by themselves, were not very comfortable, and in the early years of the system they were fed mostly loblolly, a sort of thick gruel made from Indian corn, although later the food was better.

Work in the tobacco fields was hard, and those not used to manual labor suffered the most. All had trouble working under the hot summer sun, since they were not used to Virginia's climate. Many overseers were cruel. In most colonies women did not work in the fields, but until the year 1662 in Virginia, where labor was so badly needed to plant, cultivate and harvest tobacco, women sometimes had to take their place in the fields alongside the men. There are records of women indentured servants in Virginia appearing in court to promise they would serve extra terms in order to be relieved of the field work.

At first the servants were not allowed to vote or engage in trade, and they had little chance to bring grievances before a court. They could not marry without the consent of their masters, the penalty being an extra year of servitude. In 1662 a minister who married such a couple was fined 10,000 pounds of tobacco, representing a large sum of money. Even a free person who married an indentured servant was punished by having to work a year without wages.

Later, however, Virginia changed conditions greatly for its indentured servants. They were allowed to vote, provided they paid a poll tax for the support of the government and the money known as tithes for the support of the church. To earn money for these expenditures they were allowed to trade, except with the Indians, and to own land. Animals they trapped, especially beaver, and articles fashioned of wood in their spare time could provide servants with a small income. They could bring complaints against their masters before the Virginia courts and in most cases received fair treatment. For example, if an indentured servant did not get enough food or clothing, the court might order him to be taken away from his master for a time.

A number of cases in Virginia show that it was possible for an indentured servant to obtain justice in the courts. A woman servant there complained she had been sold for a term of seven years because her indenture, which called for only four years of servitude, had been destroyed. She produced three witnesses who had seen the papers and the Virginia court ordered her set free, the four years having been completed.

Again, in 1689 two servants went to court and charged that the indentures they had signed before leaving England had been stolen from their huts. When their terms were completed, the master refused to set them free and give them their freedom dues. The court believed the two and freed them.

Black indentured servants were rare, but there is a record of one in 1691 who claimed he had been unfairly treated. It is to the credit of the Virginia court which heard his evidence that it decided in his favor, since it was long after black slavery had begun in the colony, and African slaves had no rights at all. The black man, Benjamin Lewis, told the court that he had been living in England when he signed an indenture for a four-year term in America.

His master's testimony contradicted itself. First he claimed Lewis's indenture was forged and that he should be a slave; then he brought out another indenture calling for fourteen years of servitude. Whichever document was the true one, it made Lewis an indentured servant and therefore he could not be an African slave, doomed to serve for the rest of his life. The court decided that Lewis had told the truth, that the first document was the real one, and set him free.

Yet when another servant claimed his master had forged an indenture calling for two more years of servitude than the one he had signed, the court was not convinced and sent him back to serve out the two years.

Servants obtained some benefits that they might never have received if they had not been indentured. Those who were able to survive the Virginia climate and become accustomed to it could learn much about the system of farming that the soil, climate and other conditions made necessary, as well as the ways in which agricultural products were marketed. When they were freed, these servants were better qualified to do their own farming for profit. Even some of the undesirable servants of low character profited by having to work under discipline, mended their ways and became good citizens when their terms ended.

Those who were artisans and worked at their trades on the plantations gained an advantage from their servitude. During those years they were almost certain to meet other planters in the vicinity. When they were freed they might find employment at good wages, either with their own masters or other plantation owners who could offer better jobs. The benefit of having a trade was so great that there are records in Virginia in which indentured servants agreed to serve an extra year or two for being taught a trade.

Yet even with these benefits, the servants were not free. As was the case with many black slaves, those who had cruel or stingy masters often ran away. And like the black slaves, the white ones often never were caught. Sometimes groups of them would plan a mass escape and in some cases persuade their black companions on a plantation to join them.

In the wild back country of Virginia, escape was fairly easy. If the runaways could reach the northern colonies, they were generally safe. The distance made returning them difficult. And in New England there was some disfavor against the indentured-servant system; Connecticut had no laws under which a runaway could be recovered.

The problem of runaways in Virginia was a serious one to the Virginia plantation owners. At first a runaway who was caught had his term of servitude extended one or two years. Later the amount of extra time served was left up to the master. In several cases from two to seven years were added. And anyone who caught runaways and returned them to their masters received a reward of a thousand pounds of tobacco. The value of this reward had to be returned to the plantation owner by the servant, whose term was extended still further to do so.

The decline of white servitude in Virginia began around 1726 and came practically to an end by 1788, due to the vast numbers of black slaves brought into the colony. It was much cheaper for a plantation owner to buy a black slave who must work without pay the rest of his life. Also the blacks, being from tropical Africa, could stand the work in the fields in summer much better.

Indentured white servitude in Virginia was probably worse in certain respects than in most other American colonies. Yet there were many masters who treated their indentured servants with great kindness, fed and clothed them well and when their terms were ended were generous with freedom dues. Some servants, when their terms had ended, went on to lead successful and happy lives as freemen. Some even became distinguished citizens, as will be seen later.

6

HOW THEY FARED
IN MARYLAND

In Maryland, as in Virginia, tobacco was king; little else was raised in quantity and the demand for labor in the tobacco fields was so great that these two colonies were prime markets for indentured servants, mostly from the British Isles. In the early years of settlement, Virginia's treatment of servants was probably the harshest. However, once an actual system of indentures began, Virginia was forced to relax its stiff discipline and cruel punishment. In Maryland the laws concerning indentured servants were in general not as severe, but there was much harsh treatment which appears to have continued longer than in Virginia.

Captains of ships carrying indentured servants and redemptioners to Maryland often treated their passengers viciously, both during the voyage and upon arrival. More than a hundred years after Maryland was founded, a newspaper writer there reported a voyage of unbelievable hardship and cruelty by the vessel's master.

Every two weeks at sea the passengers received an allowance of bread. One man and his wife, having eaten their bread in eight days, staggered before the captain and begged him to throw them overboard, for they would otherwise starve before the next bread day. The captain laughed in their faces, while the ship's mate, even more of a brute, gave them a bag of sand and told them to eat that. The couple did die before the next ration of bread, but the captain charged the other passengers for the bread the two would have eaten if they had survived.

Like some bound for other colonies, passengers who had embarked without indentures or had lost them or had them stolen could be sold for a longer term of servitude than their indentures would have called for. Shipmasters sometimes passed off immigrants who knew no trade as having one. A young Englishman of good family, well enough off to style himself a "gentleman," was enticed aboard a ship headed for Maryland by a spirit. The captain, seeing that he had a high-class passenger, asked him what sort of work he did. The young man replied that he was not accustomed to working at anything.

The captain said this would not do at all; his passenger must have a trade or he would find himself slaving in unbearable heat in the Maryland tobacco fields. How about declaring himself a gardener? It took no special knowledge, was easy work, and plantation owners in the colony were eager to find gardeners.

The young gentleman fell in with the scheme and the captain sold him for a handsome profit to a planter. It was not long, however, before the master discovered that his new servant had no experience at all with gardening. He was naturally disgruntled, while the young man became unhappy and dissatisfied with work he knew nothing about and began to shirk his duties. His master, a good and kindly man, tried to make the best of a bad bargain, but reprovals did no good, nor finally did threats of punishment. At last the master gave up and had his worthless gardener sentenced to the iron mines that supplied the colony's forges and mills. With the prospect of grueling labor looming ahead, the young man humbly asked his master's forgiveness.

The kind-hearted planter not only forgave him but obtained a berth for him as a steward aboard a ship bound for England. Some time passed; then one day the planter received a letter from his former gardener, who poured out his gratitude and enclosed a sum of money much larger than what the master had paid for him. The planter was delighted but decided he could not keep the money and sent it back. The young gentleman promptly returned it. The gratified planter then turned the money over to charity. Here was one instance of a Maryland planter who went beyond all bounds to help an unfortunate indentured servant.

Many were not so lucky. Even though Maryland eventually passed laws giving indentured servants the right to bring complaints of ill treatment to court, some masters got away with brutal and inhuman usage. William Eddis, who was the English surveyor of customs at Annapolis in 1770 and wrote letters home telling of conditions in Maryland, said that indentured servants in the colony "groaned beneath a worse than Egyptian bondage." It is a fact that suicide among them was fairly common.

In 1756 a Maryland indentured servant became so despondent over the treatment he was receiving that he ran away with an Indian slave also kept by his master. Evidently they went to an Indian village in the back country. The master learned where they were and sent a man to bring them back. Presumably the other Indians were ready to help the runaways, for the two sent word back that they would rather live as pagans, as the Indians were called by the whites, than to return, starve and "have their brains beat out."

Servants who took their complaints to court sometimes got little or no satisfaction. One especially unjust court decision was in the case of Sarah Taylor, a maidservant on the plantation of Captain Thomas Bradnox in Kent County, Maryland.

Since Captain Bradnox was a justice of the peace, he felt safe from punishment for brutality to his servants. It was known that when he was drunk he often beat his white servants with tobacco stalks. In Sarah Taylor's case he used a rope.

Sarah ran away. A planter who had no use for Bradnox's brutal ways gave her refuge. The captain had him summoned into court for harboring a runaway, always a serious offense in the colonies. The judges made the kindly planter ask Captain Bradnox's forgiveness in open court and promise never to do such a thing again. As for Sarah, one of the justices wanted her whipped, but the others decided the lashes she had already received were punishment enough provided she got down on her knees and asked forgiveness of Captain Bradnox and his wife, who was as cruel as he was.

Bradnox was enraged at the lenient punishments given Sarah and her planter benefactor. The captain and Mrs. Bradnox became more brutal than ever, whipping and showering abuse on Sarah for no reason. At last the wretched girl ran away again and hid in the woods until, almost starved, she crept before the county commissioners to ask justice.

She described how, while working in the kitchen, she was suddenly set upon by Bradnox and his wife. While Mrs. Bradnox held her down, the captain belabored her with a rope's end. She showed the commissioners twenty-one livid welts on her back and arms. She also brought in a witness who told how one morning Captain Bradnox seized a three-legged stool and hit Sarah over the head with it.

The commissioners ordered her set free. Captain Bradnox, infuriated at losing an indentured servant, used his influence to bring the case to the attention of the governor, who appointed two men to decide it. They were of a different stamp from the fair-minded commissioners. Since Sarah Taylor actually worked for Mrs. Bradnox, these two judges ordered each of the commissioners who had first heard the case to pay the captain's wife 220 pounds of tobacco. But at least Sarah was free, though what happened to her afterward is not known.

Other Maryland justices sometimes did deal out severe punishment to masters. Jeffrey Haggmann, an indentured servant belonging to Joseph Fincher, was found dead. Fincher was known for brutality and was charged with murder for whipping the man to death. After a great deal of evidence for and against Fincher, he was found guilty and hanged.

Another brutal master also paid for murdering a boy, Henry Gouge, who was indentured to him. Gouge's naked body was found floating in a mill-pond near Newtown, where his master, James Dandy, lived. The body was covered with black and blue marks and Dandy, too, was charged with whipping his indentured servant to death, convicted and hanged.

Religious bigotry was responsible for much persecution of servants. James Calvert, Lord Baltimore, founded Maryland in 1632 as a refuge for Catholics, who were unwanted and ill-treated in some other colonies. He established the colony with full freedom of religion. Unfortunately, a good many narrow-minded Puritans also settled there and in time grew so powerful that in the seventeenth century they seized control of the government. As a result, the Maryland Catholics, including indentured Catholic servants, suffered persecution.

This continued even after the Puritan regime of Cromwell ended in England. The colony became a royal province, with the official religion that of the Church of England. In 1699 the colony imposed a tax of 20 shillings on each Irish Catholic immigrant and in 1717 an additional 20 shillings was collected from arriving Irish Catholics who refused to take an oath of allegiance to the king of England and thus to the English church.

Among the Irish immigrants was a young indentured servant, Rickett Mecane, who had been a boy living in England when he was kidnaped with seven others by a spirit and shipped to Maryland. He was then about twelve, while the other boys were so much younger that someone who saw them remarked that they should have had cradles to rock them in.

Mecane was sold to Thomas Gerrard to serve for fifteen years. When he was nineteen and had served six and a half years, he submitted a petition to the governor of Maryland to be freed. Witnesses came to the young man's aid. One testified that when the boys had been sold, the ship's captain had threatened them with a whipping unless they signed indentures to serve fifteen years. Another said the boys had signed, but all were too young to know what they were doing. The provincial court decided that Mecane should be freed when he was twenty-one, after serving nine years, a doubtful sort of justice to him.

A pitiful case in which justice was finally done was that of John Ward. He also must have been kidnaped or lured by a spirit in England, for he was only nine or ten when he arrived in Maryland. Since he had no indenture, he agreed to serve Arthur Turner of Charles County until he was twenty-one. Turner did not appreciate the bargain he had obtained, for he mistreated the boy shamefully.

John Ward was nearly twenty-one when the county commissioners, hearing of his ill treatment, haled Turner into court to explain. They brought the young man in, too, and he stood before the commissioners in rags, almost naked. His legs were bared and on one was what was described in the records as "a most rotten, stinking, filthy ulcer." The commissioners set him free, but the record does not show that the brute Turner was punished otherwise.

Ward's term of servitude, like those of many others who came to Maryland without indentures, was especially long. The usual terms varied over the years. In 1639 Maryland required that all male servants over eighteen should serve for four years, which was fair enough, but those under eighteen had to serve until they were twenty-four, a grossly unfair term, since it meant that a boy of twelve, for example, must remain a slave for twelve years. Maidservants were better treated; if they were over twelve they served for four years, and under twelve, for seven.

Indentures signed in Europe for service in Maryland ordinarily called for terms of only four or five years, although there were the usual violations by unscrupulous masters who kept their servants beyond their terms, especially because of the "custom of the country" trap in many indentures.

A law of 1640 in Maryland required that when an indentured servant's term was up, the master must provide freedom dues of one new suit of broadcloth or kersey, one new shirt, one pair of new shoes and stockings and a Monmouth cap, much worn in Maryland and Virginia in colonial days, made of wool with a brim and a tasseled, peaked top that hung to one side. Also to be furnished were two hoes, an ax, three barrels of corn and fifty acres of land. Women servants got a similar amount of clothing and land and a year's supply of corn. But as happened elsewhere, some miserly masters did not comply fully with the law.

Occasionally an indentured servant with some special skill could bargain with his master to shorten his term of servitude. An unusual agreement was made in 1642 by Thomas Todd, who was indentured to John Lewger, then secretary of the Maryland province. Todd was a glover, and his master set him free on condition that every year thereafter Todd was to take a certain number of skins and prepare and fashion them into gloves and breeches for Lewger.

As in other colonies, Maryland indentured servants had few rights in the early years. They could not vote, were forbidden to marry without consent of their masters, could not leave their houses or sell any goods or property without this consent or sell their indentures to someone else if they were dissatisfied.

As time went on, these laws were relaxed to some extent. In Maryland, unlike Virginia, the demand for indentured servants continued even after the coming of black slavery, and the planters had to offer better inducements to agents abroad or ship captains to obtain white servants. In 1672 the average price for a redemptioner who had not been indentured before leaving home and was unable to pay his passage money was £10; by 1770 it had risen to £30, even though the average cost of his passage was then never over £13 and sometimes as low as £6.

The problem of runaways was as great in Maryland as in Virginia and some other colonies, and the penalties in Maryland were made more and more severe as time went on. Even as early as 1639 a Maryland law prescribed the death penalty for a captured runaway, although there is no record that it was ever enforced. However, many masters gave their returned runaway servants terrible whippings, and a runaway who was caught generally served ten extra days for each day of absence. By the eighteenth century, however, this was reduced to five days.

It was the custom in colonial days for travelers to carry a sort of passport identifying them. In fact, when Benjamin Franklin, as a young printer's apprentice, ran away from Boston in 1723 to go to Philadelphia, he wrote of being suspected on the journey as a runaway indentured servant because he had no traveler's pass. In Maryland anyone found more than ten miles from home without a pass or written permission from a master could be seized as a runaway.

This did not prevent some indentured servants from running away. Often they forged passes. One man forged a pass for himself under a false name and traveled about claiming to be trying to catch a runaway—himself!

As in Virginia, few Maryland runaways were caught. One writer who delved into the records found that out of an average of 150 advertisements each year in the weekly *Maryland Gazette* for runaways, including black slaves, only four or five a year were reported captured. Yet escaping was not easy. It was a felony for anyone to conceal a runaway, and those who caught one in Maryland and took him either to his master or to jail received a reward of 200 pounds of tobacco. However, runaways often made their way to freedom wearing clothes stolen from their masters and posing as gentleman travelers whom no one would suspect of being indentured servants.

The indentured-servant system did not die out as quickly in Maryland as in Virginia, even though black slaves replaced many white workers in the tobacco fields of both colonies. Eventually, however, it did, and the nearest thing to an indentured servant was the apprentice who signed papers to serve a master without pay for a term of years in return for being taught a trade.

7

LAND OF PROMISE,
OFTEN BROKEN

Gabriel Thomas was one of the small advance party sent to America in 1681 by William Penn to select a site for Philadelphia, the first settlement of the new colony of Pennsylvania. Penn himself and the first real colonists came in 1682. Once Philadelphia was established and began its amazingly swift growth, Thomas, like Penn, wrote a pamphlet about Pennsylvania. It was published in 1694, at a time when the need for many more settlers in Pennsylvania was acute.

Thomas described the flourishing city of Philadelphia, its beautiful situation, the fertility of Pennsylvania's soil, the clear sweetness of the air—especially attractive to dwellers in London's smoky, foggy, damp climate—the navigable rivers, the astonishing amount of corn being produced. He wrote that the colony was a paradise for poor people, since wages were three times as high as in England and Wales. Thomas gave some figures on the amounts paid carpenters to build both houses and ships, bricklayers, masons, shoemakers, tailors, weavers, tanners and curriers of leather, felt makers, glaziers, coopers, butchers, bakers, wheelwrights, millwrights, ropemakers, gunsmiths, printers and bookbinders. He said a blacksmith with one helper made the un-heard-of profit of 50 shillings a day. Moreover, food, drink and clothing were far cheaper than in England and there were no beggars to be seen.

All this was true enough. Pennsylvania was prob-ably the best-situated colony in America for indus-trial and commercial development. It had immense natural resources. West of Philadelphia rich farm-lands were being developed. They not only pro-duced food of all kinds but also flax to be spun into linen thread for household uses and clothing and hemp for rope needed to fit out the vessels that were being built from the limitless supplies of timber in nearby forests. By 1692 iron ore had been discovered and was being smelted, the beginning of what would become Pennsylvania's mighty steel industry. As for the weaving of cloth, the first settlers of German-town were from industrial Krefeld near the Rhine in Germany, known as the "City of Weavers." Irish and French settlers also were skilled in textile work.

By 1730 Pennsylvania was exporting wheat, flour, biscuit, barreled beef, hams, pork, bacon, cheese, butter, apple cider, beer, beeswax, leather, linseed oil, skins of several kinds and tobacco, although Pennsylvania never rivaled Maryland and Virginia in that crop. Ships to carry all these products were built, and before 1730 there were sometimes as many as twenty at once on the building stocks in Philadelphia, some of them big, three-masted, full-rigged ships, barks and barkentines. Smaller vessels were also built, many to be sold in the West Indies.

No wonder there was such a tremendous demand for labor in Pennsylvania in the late seventeenth century and during the eighteenth. Also, when black slavery commenced in America, public opinion in Pennsylvania, especially among its many Quakers, was so strongly against it that the colony's need for white servants continued to be great.

But Gabriel Thomas's glowing description of Pennsylvania did not include the difficulties of reaching Philadelphia or, once there, the hardships that so many immigrants would face.

The sufferings of the Germans and Swiss in getting to America were described by Gottfried Mittelberger in his account of the frightful transatlantic voyage, as well as the troubles these immigrants faced on arrival at Philadelphia. Mittelberger remained in Pennsylvania nearly four years, and although he did have good things to say about the life of some colonists there, he also wrote of the miseries he observed among indentured servants and redemptioners. He described how many German immigrants wished they had never left home and pleaded with him, tearfully and in the name of God, to warn those who had remained in their homeland of the misery and sorrow they would escape if they stayed in Germany. Mittelberger wrote: "I say that those who suffer themselves to be persuaded and enticed away by the man-thieves are very foolish, for they believe that roasted pigeons will fall into their mouths in America or Pennsylvania without working for them."

Mittelberger described the case of a man named Daser from his own native duchy of Württemberg who was not an indentured servant or redemptioner, but ran afoul of the system before he had been long in Pennsylvania. Daser was in comfortable circumstances when he left Germany with his wife and eight children. He paid 600 florins for the whole family's passage but during the voyage was robbed of goods worth 1,800 florins.

The family arrived in Philadelphia in wretched condition. Daser appears to have made connections in Philadelphia that enabled him to borrow money to buy a plantation, but the lenders turned out to be swindlers. Not being familiar with English, Daser thought when he signed a note for the loan that he was agreeing to repay the money in two years. To his horror he found that the note called for repayment in two days! Worse, he had not received a penny of the money, nor did he have any proof that it had not been paid him.

Daser was faced with either going to a debtors'

prison, where he would stay until he paid the money he had never received, or else selling his children to be indentured, but this latter he would not do at the time. Meanwhile, all the possessions he had left were sold at public auction for a trifling sum, which went as part payment to the swindlers.

The courageous man was not beaten. He brought a suit against the English shipping company, claiming it was responsible for the theft during the voyage. Meanwhile, he found a friend in Philadelphia in a Captain Diemer, who provided him and his family with food, money and lodging while the suit was going on.

Again Daser had ill luck. He lost his case against the shipping company, and this meant he had to pay all the court costs. He was despondent now and half out of his mind. The one thing that could keep him from prison was slavery for some of his children. He gave up then and sold his two eldest daughters and eldest son under indentures for three-year terms of servitude in order to save himself and the rest of his family. What happened after that Mittelberger did not know, since he was then about to return to Germany. It is to be hoped that Daser was able to find employment and that in time all his family were reunited.

Other immigrants into Pennsylvania were victimized by a class of speculators who in their way were as bad as the spirits of England and the newlanders of Germany. They were called "soul-drivers." When a ship arrived in Philadelphia from Europe, the soul-drivers would board her, buy up about fifty immigrants and drive them like cattle out of the city and through the countryside, stopping at farms and selling them for as much as each would bring. In time the soul-drivers got such a bad name that public opinion forced them out of business and by about 1758 they had disappeared.

One soul-driver got a just reward for his cruel business. Among a lot of immigrants he bought was a sharp-witted Irishman who decided to pay off his captor in his own coin. By some slick maneuvering he managed to appear to be an undesirable purchase at each place the soul-driver stopped. Finally he was the only one left unsold.

That night the two put up at a tavern. Early the next morning the Irishman got up while the soul-driver was still sleeping. He talked to the landlord, who was also up early making preparations to serve breakfast to his guests in the tavern. Representing himself as the soul-driver, the Irishman told the innkeeper that since the immigrant still asleep upstairs was the last of the lot he would sell him at a bargain price. The landlord, needing help in the inn, agreed.

In order to avoid quick pursuit, the Irishman explained that while the landlord's purchase was an excellent worker, he was not always truthful and often made up false tales. In fact, the supposed soul-driver added, this immigrant had had the audacity at one farm to try to pass himself off as the owner of the others and even of the Irishman himself.

The Irishman pocketed the money the landlord paid him and took off at top speed. When the soul-driver came downstairs, demanding to know where his captive was, the landlord accused him of lying by falsely posing as the soul-driver who had just sold him. By the time the innkeeper was convinced that he had been defrauded, the Irishman was far away, safe from capture.

Soul-drivers, agents and captains of ships arriving in Philadelphia often heartlessly broke up families, selling one member here and another there. Occasionally, however, sometimes miraculously, members of a family who had been separated were reunited. One such case, especially amazing, happened in Philadelphia.

A man there who had been separated from his family some years before had worked out his term of servitude, was able to establish himself in business and prospered. Either he was unmarried or a widower; at any rate he decided to get an elderly couple to take care of his house. Since masters of servants often sold their indentures, the man was able to buy those of a man, his wife and daughter. When they arrived he was overjoyed to find he had purchased his own father, mother and sister.

One good thing was done for hapless German

immigrants in Philadelphia. A group of well-to-do German settlers formed the German Society of Philadelphia in 1764. They provided assistance to unfortunate arrivals from Germany and as far as possible saw to it that they were not cheated in signing indentures. The society was a bright spot for these wretched people in an otherwise dismal situation.

In spite of the benevolent system of government in Pennsylvania set up by William Penn, once the indentured-servant system began, punishment for those of them who broke the law was more severe than for freemen. One of the most shocking incidents took place in Westmoreland County in the southwestern Pennsylvania border country, less civilized than the eastern part of the colony.

There a man pleaded guilty to stealing, one of the more serious offenses known as felonies. He was sentenced to thirty-nine lashes at the public whipping post. His ears were cut off and nailed to the pillory. The pillory, fastened to an upright post, was a board made in two sections that could be separated so that the culprit's head and hands could be put through holes bored along the line of separation and the two sections then brought together and locked, holding the standing person fast. The convicted man had to stand in the pillory for an hour, where he was the target for rotten fruit, eggs, stones and the jeers of spectators. This same offender had to return the stolen goods and pay a fine of £20. But a freeman convicted of such an offense was most unlikely to suffer such severe punishment.

In 1751 Pennsylvania passed a law under which for certain offenses a freeman paid £5 for the first one and £10 for any others committed later. But for the same offenses an indentured servant or a black slave received twenty-one lashes at the public whipping post and then served three days in the workhouse on bread and water. For further offenses the sentence was thirty-one lashes and six days at hard labor.

As in other colonies, indentured servants could not marry without the master's permission; in Pennsylvania a servant who did so had a whole year added to his term of servitude. A freeman who married a servant paid a £12 fine and had to serve the colony for a year without pay; a freewoman had to pay £6 and serve a year.

Persons found wandering about who could not show proof that they were free were considered to be runaway servants. Often they were seized and jailed, and if no one came to claim them they were sold into servitude to pay the prison charges. In 1740 more than forty persons found wandering about were taken, put in jail and advertised for sale in the newspapers, usually with a line reading: "Thought to be runaway servants." Overseers of the poor often made a profit for themselves by selling inmates of the workhouses as servants.

Pennsylvania, like other colonies, had its runaway problem. A runaway who was caught had five days added to his servitude for each day of absence. Two indentured servants in Chester County fell in love but, not having their master's permission, ran away and got married. After thirteen days' absence they were captured. The court gave them thirty extra days of service for running away, five months more for the £9 it cost their master to get them back, and a year's extra servitude for their marriage. Occasionally captured runaways had to wear heavy iron collars marked with their master's initials, in case they tried to escape again.

Following the English custom, in the early years of Pennsylvania's settlement debt was a crime. Often freemen who owed money they could not pay sold themselves into servitude to avoid going to prison. Those who refused to do so could be sold anyway by the county courts—unmarried persons under the age of fifty-three for servitude of not over seven years; married people not over forty-six for not more than five years.

Because of Longfellow's famous poem "Evangeline," many people think that when the British conquered Acadia (today Nova Scotia) in 1755, the French-speaking Acadians who refused to take an oath of allegiance to the King of England were all deported to Louisiana. However, many were sent to other American colonies, more than 400 of them to

Pennsylvania. There they were treated well and provided with food, shelter and clothing, but because they spoke only French, finding work for them was a problem. There is no proof that any were sold as servants, but there is evidence that many were offered indentures, though not forced to sign.

Pennsylvania had its convict problem too. Convicts preferred to be sent there because there were far fewer crimes for which they could be executed than in other colonies. A good many were shipped from England to Pennsylvania, though apparently not as many as to Maryland and Virginia. Nevertheless, Pennsylvania was alarmed. During the 1721–22 legislative session laws were passed placing an import duty of £5 on every convict arriving in Philadelphia, and whoever brought a convict in had to post a bond of £50 to insure his good behavior for a year. Most convicts did not stay long in Philadelphia, but the people were warned against them while they remained in the city.

Once a Pennsylvania indentured servant's term was up, his freedom dues were much like those in other colonies. In 1682, the year the colony was founded, fifty acres of land, one new suit, ten bushels of wheat or fourteen of corn, one ax and two hoes were promised. In 1700 one more suit of clothes was added, though it did not have to be new. But in 1771, when the need for indentured servants had slackened, the hoes were left out of the freedom dues.

Much of this description of what happened to indentured servants and redemptioners in Pennsylvania makes life for them in the colony seem no more attractive than in others. Yet all in all, prospects for these servants in Pennsylvania were probably better than in any other colony. One reason is that Pennsylvania's industry and trade made more well-paying jobs available to freed indentured servants.

Another reason is that so many Germans came; by the beginning of the American Revolution about half of Pennsylvania's population was estimated to be German. These immigrants were chiefly hard-working, law-abiding people who served out their terms and then established themselves either as farmers in today's so-called Pennsylvania Dutch country ("Dutch" was corrupted from *Deutsch*, the German word for "German") or as artisans or household servants in Philadelphia and other Pennsylvania cities. A great many of them were sold to good masters; the cruel owners were in the minority. And as in other colonies, mistreated servants could take complaints to court.

Thus a large number of indentured servants in Pennsylvania, not only the Germans and German-speaking Swiss but those from other nations, lived to become prosperous and in some cases influential in government and politics. In fact, Gottfried Mittelberger, during his stay in Pennsylvania, found that even many of those still serving out their indentures fared well. He wrote: "An English servant-woman, especially in Philadelphia, is as elegantly dressed as an aristocratic lady in Germany."

Pennsylvania and Delaware, from about 1682 until the formation of the United States of America, were practically one colony. William Penn claimed Delaware as part of this colony, and although it did establish its own assembly in 1704, Delaware until it became a state had the same governor and council as Pennsylvania. What has been written about the indentured-servant system in Pennsylvania applies equally well to Delaware.

8

SERVANTS IN THE
SOUTHERNMOST COLONIES

North Carolina and South Carolina, sister colonies, were settled at about the same time and often lumped together as the Carolinas in those early days, but as far as indentured servitude went, they differed greatly from each other. Each had the problem of attracting settlers, but each solved it by its own method.

No exact date can be set for the original establishment of the colony of North Carolina. It began in about 1653 when some Virginians settled in the northeastern part of what is now North Carolina but was then considered Virginia territory. In 1663 King Charles II of England granted a large area south of Virginia to eight prominent Englishmen who had aided him in gaining the throne after the years in which first Oliver Cromwell and then his son Richard ruled England. The region, which included that in which the Virginians had settled in about 1653, was named Carolina in honor of the king (*Carolus* is the Latin word for Charles).

From then on, for several years, Virginians drifted southward into what was to become North Carolina. In England the eight proprietors of Carolina tried to persuade people there to come to the new colony. They held out the enticement of a hundred acres of land free, with no taxes to pay for a year. After that, quitrents, the small sum of money paid each year by freemen to the governments of most American colonies, would be kept low in Carolina.

But few colonists came from England and early settlement was confined to what later became North Carolina. It was not because the region lacked natural resources. The soil was fertile, and there were vast forests, especially of pine, which was later to be one of North Carolina's principal sources of revenue; the region teemed with fur-bearing animals and its streams with fish. But it was a great, completely undeveloped wilderness, and development was hindered by a coastline that offered few good harbors where sea trade could be established. So only a scattering of settlers came, and indentured servitude was unknown. And there were no settlements at all in South Carolina until 1669.

By that time the eight proprietors of Carolina in England had decided to see what could be done about colonizing the southern part of their vast grant and obtaining some profit from it. Late in 1669 three ships carrying colonists sailed for South Carolina. The proprietors had offered 150 acres of land to every freeman coming before March 1670, as well as 150 acres more for every able manservant he brought with him and 100 acres for every woman and for every manservant under the age of sixteen.

Two of the ships were ill-fated. Either the three headed first for the West Indies or were blown off course in a storm, for two of them were wrecked on the islands to the south. The third vessel, the *Carolina*, finally arrived at her destination in March 1670, and a colony was established at the mouth of the Ashley River. They named it Charles Town. It had a splendid harbor, which was to be one important reason for South Carolina's growth and prosperity.

A passenger list for the *Carolina* names sixteen persons. They were presumably "gentlemen" who brought servants with them, probably mostly indentured. If so, this was the beginning of indentured servitude in South Carolina. The colony's records contain one indenture, that of a woman, Millicent Howe. The document does not specify any definite term of servitude but simply says it was to be "according to the lawes and Customes and Orders for servants which are to be provided in such place." Since these were the first of South Carolina's indentured servants and thus no such "lawes and Customes" had been established, how long Millicent and the others had to serve before gaining their freedom is not known.

A clue to it turns up a little later, however. In 1770 the *Carolina* sailed for Barbados in the West Indies. In that British island she loaded more colonists, also accompanied by indentured servants. Their servitude varied from eighteen months to three years, more liberal terms than in most American colonies. Some of them were artisans—a sawyer, carpenter, farmer and woman servant are mentioned in the records.

Emigration from Barbados to South Carolina was popular. Many who came to trade with the Indians —for some years the principal activity in the Carolinas—brought with them indentured servants and also black slaves. Thus black slavery and white servitude began at about the same time in South Carolina.

At first the need for indentured servants was greater than for black slaves, however. The gentleman settlers did little but trade for furs with the Indians. They made money, but since there was little agriculture at first, there was not enough food to supply the new colony. Immigration was increasing, not only from Barbados, but from England as well. In less than a month 500 people who were fleeing religious persecution came to South Carolina from England. A large number of Protestant Huguenots who had left Roman Catholic France for this reason had taken refuge in England. When poverty forced them to leave there, they came to South Carolina. Even some Puritans from New England moved

94

south to warmer South Carolina. In two years the colony's population doubled, from about 1,100 to 2,200.

All these settlers had to be fed and South Carolina could not do it. For a time the proprietors in England sent ships with food to keep the colonists from starving. But the owners soon decided they were not getting a fair share of the profits from the Indian fur trade and also complained that quitrents were not being paid. They stopped sending food.

When suitable arrangements that satisfied the proprietors were made, food shipments were resumed. But the South Carolina settlers now realized that they must raise more crops. The luckiest thing that ever happened to them was the arrival of a ship from Madagascar in the Indian Ocean with a cargo of rice.

South Carolina's rich, marshy lowlands near the coast and along the rivers were ideal for raising rice. Soon a great many landowners were planting it. It was not only the colony's salvation but its fortune. Rice made South Carolina very prosperous.

All this had a powerful effect on the indentured-servant system. Few of the white servants were used to work in the fields; that was done by the black slaves who were imported in increasing numbers. But with the colony's new wealth came a greatly increased demand for indentured white servants as well. In the flourishing seaport that was originally

Charles Town (but now moved a short distance to a better location along the harbor and called Charleston), as well as in other towns which had been established, artisans and mechanics were needed and indentured servants with a knowledge of clerical work for merchants' countinghouses. Both in the towns and on the rice plantations whites worked as house servants and in the rice fields as overseers of the black laborers.

The great need for indentured servants who had trades is shown by the arrival of the ship *Eagle* from Holland, loaded with Germans and German-speaking Swiss. Those among them who were over fourteen and were farmers brought the high price of £36 apiece, but those who knew trades sold for higher amounts and secured shorter terms of servitude, terms which in general were less than those in other colonies and varied from one and a half to three years.

Practically every type of artisan or mechanic was certain to be sold immediately. Advertisements in the newspapers announced arrivals of immigrant ships and listed the occupations of trained indentured servants on board, including bakers, ship carpenters, cabinetmakers, joiners, bricklayers, painters, millers, sawyers, wheelwrights, ropemakers, stonecutters, barkeepers, chimney sweeps, collectors, farmers, sailors, wigmakers, gardeners, file cutters, nail makers, fencing masters (expert swordsmen had an advantage in the duels often fought between southern gentlemen) and teachers.

Fear also inspired Carolina residents to obtain servants who could be used to fight invading ene-mies. Although trade with the Indians had been of the greatest importance in the early years of settle-ment, a number of tribes had become hostile as they saw their lands and hunting grounds being taken by the whites.

Some of the tribes fought fiercely for what be-longed to them, raiding isolated settlements in the border country. In 1711 an attack by the Tuscarora tribe upon New Burn, North Carolina, almost an-nihilated the settlement; in return the whites of the Carolinas and Virginia sent an expedition against the Tuscaroras and defeated them so badly that those who were not killed fled northward and even-tually joined the powerful Five Nations of the New York colony, making them the Six Nations. Throughout the colonial period and later, the story of how the red men were first victimized and then driven from their lands is a disgraceful part of American history.

The Spaniards, who held Florida until 1763, were no friends of the English settlers north of them. They were not only hostile themselves, but also in-fluenced the Indians to attack English settlements.

In 1715 four tribes, the Yamassees, Creeks, Catawbas and Cherokees, egged on by the Spaniards, invaded the Carolinas but were finally driven out.

Black slaves could not always be depended upon when such attacks took place. They had little reason to risk their lives for their masters, and many a runaway slave had found refuge among the Indian tribes. But the more white indentured servants a planter had, the more likely he was to feel safe from the Indians and Spaniards. When an expedition against the whites' enemies had to be organized, the white servants were used as fighting men.

Moreover, southern colonists lived in dread lest their black slaves rise in rebellion to avenge their unjust and cruel slavery and gain freedom. As black slaves took over the toil in the rice fields and the newer agricultural trade of raising indigo, every planter wanted indentured servants to help keep the blacks in check.

As a result, in 1721 South Carolina passed a law to encourage still further the importation of indentured servants. Every master who bought them received a bounty of £5 for each one. By 1722 there were so many black slaves in the colony that the government voted to tax plantation owners according to the number of slaves they owned rather than on the value of their land and property, in the hope of limiting the black population somewhat.

By 1725 a law had been enacted requiring that

every person owning ten or more black slaves must have at least one white servant. The following year the requirement was one white for every ten blacks, and in 1739 a planter had to have one white servant if he owned 4,000 acres and another for each additional 2,000 acres up to 20,000 acres. Above 20,-000 acres it was one more white for each additional 1,000 acres.

South Carolina did not want convicts. The law of 1712, while encouraging ownership of indentured servants, prohibited all who had ever been in prison or jail. Anyone bringing in a convict was to be fined £25. Yet some were smuggled in. There is one record of eighteen men and seven women, all sentenced to seven years in prison for felony, who were landed in South Carolina.

As had happened in other colonies, some political prisoners were shipped in from England. In 1715 Scots known as Jacobites started a rebellion in an attempt to gain the English throne for James Edward Stuart, son of the deposed King James II of England. The rebellion was crushed and the British government paid a bounty of £30 each for thirty captured Highland rebels and indentured them for seven years of servitude in South Carolina. Those who refused to sign the indentures were shipped over anyway, and their buyers were given certificates stating that they must serve the seven years.

South Carolina also received its quota of Acadians

in the 1750s, but they were looked upon with suspicion and fear. The colony was strongly Protestant and the people felt that these French Catholics might stir up trouble among the slaves and the Indians.

The Acadians were divided into groups so that they could not form a large body of troublemakers. Only about fifty were allowed to stay in Charleston; the others were distributed among the districts called parishes into which the colony was divided. As in other colonies, the Acadians were received as refugees and were not at first required to sign indentures. But in South Carolina, too, the language problem made it difficult to place the Acadians in acceptable paying jobs. The cost of caring for them finally brought about the passage of a law in 1756 requiring that the refugees be indentured so that they could be put at the sort of labor where the language barrier did not matter so much.

While North Carolina never had as many indentured servants as its sister colony just to the south, it did want them and was able to obtain a fair number. But conditions there were so unfavorable in the early days that there are few records of the immigration of white servants. In the 1730s North Carolina was probably the most thinly settled of the American colonies.

North Carolina was not as liberal as some colonies in its efforts to attract indentured servants, presumably because it was less prosperous. In the colony's early days it offered fifty acres of land, with one penny quitrent to be paid each year after a servant's term of indenture was completed. In 1715 three barrels of Indian corn and two new suits worth at least £5 were added to the freedom dues. And North Carolina offered to those who signed indentures a reward known as "proclamation money"—the sum of £3 along with a suit of clothes.

By comparison, South Carolina in 1717 was offering better freedom dues. In addition to land, corn, an ax and a hoe, freed male servants were to be given one good coat of broadcloth or kersey, a new white linen shirt and a pair of shoes and stockings, while women got a waistcoat, petticoat, white linen chemise, new shoes and stockings, a blue apron and two white caps.

Nor was North Carolina as generous as other colonies in what planters offered when they bought arriving indentured servants. One record indicates what was paid in the case of a ship captain who brought Irishmen to North Carolina. He exchanged them for pitch or turpentine, which at that time made the value of each servant £6 or £7. It must be remembered that Irish indentured servants were considered among the least valuable of immigrants, yet at the same time South Carolina was paying far higher rates for its servants and in Maryland even convicts were bought for from £8 to £20 apiece.

Though North Carolina raised tobacco, its production did not rival that of Virginia and Maryland in colonial days. In the eighteenth century it was the great pine forests, from which came naval stores—tar, pitch, resin and turpentine—as well as timber, that provided North Carolina with its greatest revenue. This industry might have enabled the colony to attract more indentured servants but for the introduction of black slavery, which provided the colony with labor for the forests and tobacco fields. The skill of artisans and mechanics was less needed in North than in South Carolina, where trade and industry were flourishing, and North Carolina never had a vast number of white servants.

Runaways plagued the Carolinas like their neighboring colonies. In South Carolina a law of 1668 provided for adding twenty-eight days to a captured runaway's servitude, and in 1673 the penalty was nearly doubled. Punishment became even harsher in 1717, when one week was added to a returned runaway's term for each day of absence. In 1744 captured ones were driven through the parishes where they lived and whipped as they went along.

Perhaps the most fantastic story of a runaway indentured servant is that of Sarah Wilson, an extremely clever woman and a thief. She came originally from London, where she was a maidservant to Lady Grosvenor, a maid of honor to King George III's wife, Queen Charlotte. Sarah came to know the royal apartments in the palace well. One day when no one was about she looted a cabinet of many valuable jewels and fled.

Sarah Wilson was caught and tried and sentenced to death, but Lady Grosvenor took pity on her and pleaded with the queen for the young woman's life. Instead of being hanged, she was transported to Maryland and sold as an indentured servant.

Sarah's narrow escape changed neither her thieving ways nor her artfulness. She had managed to hide some of the stolen jewels and smuggled them into Maryland with her, along with the fine clothes she had worn as one of the palace staff. She soon ran away from her Maryland master and, because she was so well dressed, had no trouble in posing as a lady of quality. Presumably she sold a few of the stolen jewels to pay her traveling expenses.

Sarah Wilson moved southward through Virginia and North Carolina to South Carolina. There she announced that she was Princess Susanna Carolina Matilda, sister of Queen Charlotte, visiting the American colonies. She exhibited a stolen picture of the queen to prove her royal lineage.

The smartly dressed, bejeweled Sarah made a great success with her false claim. At plantation after plantation she was welcomed. Many did her homage by kissing her hand. In return for gifts of money she made extravagant promises of royal favor once she returned to England.

After a time, however, some people with keen minds began to suspect a hoax. In some way word of her presence in South Carolina reached her master in Maryland and he dispatched a messenger who seized and took her back to servitude.

What happened to Sarah Wilson after that is not known. She was undoubtedly suitably punished by her master and served out her term along with a lengthy time added to her servitude. But if she was eventually freed, a woman of her talents would surely have managed to do well, honestly or dishonestly.

The Carolinas, like other colonies, had their harsh masters and their kind ones. Some were generous beyond what the law required in freedom dues when an indentured servant's term expired. Often they added extra goods or money. Some gave their servants freedom before their servitude was completed.

A number of masters who died did not forget their indentured servants in their wills. For example, in South Carolina, Francis Le Brasseur left his white servant boy, Jacob Marki, £15 in South Carolina currency and directed the executors of his will to put the boy in school to learn reading and writing. Another master, William Roos, owned a favorite maidservant who still had three years to serve when he died. He bequeathed her the indentures she had signed, making her a free woman. Still another, Jacob Roth, left his servant girl, Anna Apleonya, her conditional release; if his wife died before the maidservant's time was up she was to go free. In the meantime, the girl was to have her choice of either a cow with a calf or a mare and a colt, which she could then sell for a substantial sum of money.

The most generous of masters mentioned in the South Carolina records were Alexander Vander Dusen and John Summers. Vander Dusen, evidently a rich man, left £1,000 to his manservant, Charles Murrine; to a young maidservant went the same amount, to be invested, with the interest going to her and the whole amount to be paid when she either married or reached the age of twenty-one. Summers left not only his entire estate to his maidservant, Sara, and her children but also one black slave to her and one to each of her children.

In the history of the indentured-servant system, Georgia can almost be ignored. It was the last of the American colonies to be settled, in 1733. James Oglethorpe founded Georgia as a refuge for deserving poor people of England who were of good character, many of them freed from debtors' prisons to come to America after they had been carefully investigated. Oglethorpe intended that Georgia should be wholly Protestant, but when three London Jews collected enough money to send forty of their faith to Georgia, Oglethorpe let them stay.

Most of the Georgia immigrants had their passage paid by Oglethorpe and his group of trustees who oversaw the colony, but some indentured servants did come, although how many is not known. The trustees appointed a man to assemble a shipload of them in the Scottish Highlands and also had agents in Holland and the Lower Rhineland recruiting servants. One shipment of immigrants is known to have been sold for the low price of £4 each, so their terms of servitude were probably short, and the records indicate that the trustees provided a generous allowance of food while they were at sea during the ocean voyage.

South Carolina stands out as the principal market for indentured servants in the southernmost colonies during the last years of the seventeenth century and into the eighteenth. North Carolina, although it needed them, developed too slowly to attract many before black slavery practically did away with the need. Georgia, so different in the way it was colonized, played a very small part in the indentured-servant system.

9

NEW YORK, THE PALATINE
FIASCO AND NEW JERSEY

While the New York colony was held by its original settlers, the Dutch, it was operated under the patroon system. The patroons were mostly wealthy Hollanders who received large grants of land and established plantations in New Netherland, as the colony was then called. Although they were under Dutch authority, the patroons were like petty kings on their great estates and ran things to suit themselves. It was practically a feudal system under which the farmer-settlers on these estates paid rent for the land they occupied, but were exempt from taxes for ten years.

The tenants' farms were often large and they needed labor to help them raise crops, so the Dutch government sent them indentured servants. The so-called "free-willers" who emigrated by their own choice were mostly good workers, but the tenant farmers also had to take paupers and convicts released from prison and transported to America, as well as many young children from the almshouses maintained for the poor in Amsterdam. The number of acres a patroon owned determined the number of indentured servants he had.

Free-willers came without signing indentures before leaving and were at the mercy of the ship's captain, who sold them for the longest possible terms of servitude, often for seven years, in order to make the largest profit he could. Although convicts were not generally liked, they were also in some demand because they, too, were indentured for seven years. Redemptioners who had paid part of their passage money before sailing were indentured for five years if they could not pay what they still owed on landing.

In 1664 the English captured the town of New Amsterdam and took over the rule of the colony, changing its name from New Netherland to New York. They continued the patroon system in a somewhat different way, granting large tracts of land to English gentlemen who were known as "lords of the manor." The number of acres granted each lord depended upon the number of indentured servants he brought with him.

However, the New York colony failed to take full advantage of its indentured servants to develop agricultural and industrial prosperity, as Pennsylvania had. In general, indentured servants were poorly treated in New York. And the one important attempt the colony, assisted by England, made to bring in a large number of them was a dismal failure. It was called the Palatine project.

This plan did not begin as an indentured-servant system but was simply an effort by the British government to get rid of some of a horde of German emigrants who were waiting in London and its vicinity for passage to America. In 1708 a group from the Rhineland Palatinate was sent to New York and settled about fifty miles north of New York City on the west bank of the Hudson River. They named the settlement Palatinate Parish by Quassaic; it has become today's city of Newburgh. The Palatines caused nothing but trouble for the New York colony's government, which, with the later assistance of two colonial officials, had to support the German settlers for a year until they were able to establish farms and raise enough crops to support themselves.

The British government had planned to have these colonists produce tar, pitch and other naval stores, but the settlers did nothing about the project, nor did either the royal or colonial governments take steps to get it started. Apparently the London authorities thought no plans or special preparations were necessary for this complicated process. The Palatines settled down to farming on the land granted them.

However, the British government had not forgotten the plan to produce naval stores. It decided to send an even larger group of Palatines to the Hudson Valley. This time they intended to see to it that the settlers got to work on the project.

Ten ships loaded with 2,814 Palatines sailed from London in January 1710. These people were indentured, but in a most unusual fashion—not to New York owners but to Queen Anne of England herself. They were free-willers who had come to England by their own choice, expecting that the government would arrange for their passage to America.

The Palatines signed an agreement before leaving. Under it they promised to settle on lands assigned to them and produce naval stores; they would not stop production or leave without permission from the government of New York. The agreement also included the promise "that as soon as we shall have made good and repaid to her Majesty, her heirs and successors out of the produce of our labours . . . the full sum or sums of money to which we already are or shall become indebted to her Majesty," the governor was to grant to each Palatine "forty acres of land free of all quitrents or other manner of services for seven years."

The language of the final part of the agreement is not fully clear, but it appears that the Palatines were to work off their indebtedness to the queen before receiving their grants of forty acres of land. They would then also be freemen. Yet the clause about the land was to cause much dissension among the Palatines.

The Palatines' voyage from London was a long one, for the ships stopped off, presumably to load additional supplies and water, first at Portsmouth and then at Plymouth along the English Channel. Before the first of the vessels arrived in New York, her passengers had been aboard nearly six months; about eight months aboard was the time for those in the last ship to reach port.

The voyage was different from the comparatively easy time the Palatines had enjoyed coming down the Rhine and journeying from Rotterdam to London. Their sufferings during the passage were much like those described by Gottfried Mittelberger in 1750. They were closely packed into the ships, and the stench below decks, where most of them were, became sickening. The passengers were infested with vermin, and they got little fresh air and saw no daylight in those dark holds. Many died, especially the young children; before the end of July 446 had perished, although the loss was somewhat offset by the birth of thirty children during the crossing.

The first ship, the *Lyon*, arrived in New York on June 13, 1710. Several others reached port the next day, but as so often happened, bad weather had scattered the vessels during the voyage and it was August before the last one put into port. One, the

Herbert, never got there at all. She was wrecked on the eastern end of Long Island, though apparently her passengers were landed safely.

No warm welcome awaited the Palatines in New York City. The people, learning of the conditions aboard the ships, were afraid the Palatines would endanger their health; in fact, some of the Germans were then ill with the dread disease of typhus. The New York City Council solved the problem by temporarily settling the immigrants on Governor's Island, off the tip of Manhattan Island where New York City was then centered.

The council also took care of another problem. The parents of seventy-four young children had died during the voyage. The youngsters were indentured as apprentices to mechanics and artisans in the city, where they would learn a trade.

Among these indentured orphans was John Peter Zenger, who was destined to become famous. He was then fourteen and was apprenticed to a printer in New York City for eight years. He eventually gained his freedom and in 1733 started the *New York Weekly Journal.* Articles critical of the governor were contributed by leading New Yorkers opposed to his way of government. As the publisher of the articles, Zenger was arrested and held in jail ten months awaiting trial. But in August 1735, after being defended by a notable lawyer who volunteered his services, Zenger was acquitted by a jury. It was the first important victory for freedom of the press in America.

While the orphaned children were being disposed of, the New York government was trying to decide where to settle the Palatines. Among the proposed sites was a gift of land from the Mohawk Indian tribe in the Schoharie Valley west of Albany, but the plan was abandoned when it was found that there were no pitch pines there.

Finally a distinguished and wealthy New Yorker, Robert Livingston, sold the government 6,000 acres of his vast estate, Livingston Manor, on the east side of the Hudson River. Close by was a large tract of pitch pines, and Livingston granted the privilege of using it for producing naval stores. Another tract on the opposite side of the river was also bought for the use of the Palatines.

By October 1710 the settlers were moving north up the Hudson Valley. Three towns were established on the Livingston Manor purchase and two on the west side of the river. While the Germans were building rough log huts plastered with mud, Livingston supplied them with tents, tools and other necessities. More Palatines arrived, and by June 1711 there were seven villages in the area. Later still more were established.

Life for the indentured servants was not pleasant. Winter was close at hand and no crops could be started until spring. The food they were given was scanty. Thus it is not strange that Livingston's own storehouses of grain were robbed, nor difficult to figure out who did it, since soon afterward the Palatines asked permission to bake their own bread. The settlers were short of many necessities—steel for mending edged tools, tools for a blacksmith shop, millstones to grind grain, the long, narrow whipsaws used for cutting timber, plowshares, pitchforks, nails, iron for horseshoes and harness for the horses used to haul timber.

Much of this equipment was needed for the main project of producing naval stores. The New York authorities went about organizing and carrying out the project in the poorest possible way. For one thing, Colonel Robert Hunter, then governor of New York and in charge of the work, put a military organization into effect. The Germans were so indignant at being treated like soldiers, marched to work and strictly disciplined, that a large group rose in rebellion. The New York government swiftly controlled them by establishing even harsher military measures.

The Palatines retaliated by forming a secret association of those determined not to stay on the Livingston Manor project. They claimed they had been cheated because they should have received their forty acres apiece at once, although the language of the agreement seems fairly clear that the land would be theirs only after they had worked off their debts to the queen and British government. They presented a demand that they be given "the lands appointed them by the Queen" in the Schoharie Valley. It was excellent, fertile land which the Germans, expert farmers, could easily develop. As for the naval stores project, they wanted no more of it.

Governor Hunter acted swiftly to show the Palatines he would stand for no such nonsense. He sent a military detachment of seventy men from Albany to march on the Palatine villages. The Germans had some weapons, but the soldiers seized them and Hunter had the settlers at his mercy. The people then asked his pardon and appeared to be ready to start making naval stores.

If Hunter had accepted their apology in good faith, things might have gone somewhat better. Instead, he put into effect extremely hard punishments for relatively small misdemeanors. Also, distribution of supplies to the Palatines was badly handled; several days or a week would pass without food or supplies, and often there was not enough to be distributed to all the villages, and the quality was poor. Hunter was not entirely to blame, however, for the supply problem. He had already spent £21,700 on the Palatines, £19,200 of it for food, and he was having financial difficulties.

The governor had another problem on his hands. He wanted no delay in starting production of naval stores and hired a man from New England who was well qualified to handle the job. But before production could start, the man asked permission to return to New England for the winter and come back in the spring. When spring came he appears to have been dissatisfied with the salary offered him and refused to return.

Governor Hunter then engaged Richard Sackett, a farmer of the Livingston Manor region, to take charge of the work. It was a poor solution, for Sackett did not have the proper experience and qualifications to handle the rather complicated process.

First, the trees had to be barked—that is, a part of the bark on the lower section of the tree trunk peeled off. The method then in use was to peel a strip from the ground up about eight feet, leaving a narrow strip of bark on the tree's north side. The barked tree was then allowed to stand in this condition for at least a year, sometimes two or three for the best results. Meanwhile, the tarry resin in the tree would settle in the peeled part of the trunk.

When the trees were ready for extraction of the resin, they were cut down, usually in winter. The part that had been barked was sawn off and split into sections about the thickness of a man's arm and stacked in piles about six feet high. Then the sections were heated slowly in one of the crude kilns or ovens then used, but not allowed to burn.

In this heating and sweating process the resin flowed slowly out of the wood and into a trench alongside the kiln. From it turpentine could be distilled and the residue used for the tar and pitch needed for caulking the seams of the wooden warships built for the British navy and other vessels. The process was a wasteful one because the pitch pine trees used were destroyed. This later gave way to the more modern method by which the trees are preserved.

Richard Sackett had different ideas about how to bark the pitch pines, but his method failed to produce good results. Although about 100,000 trees were barked, only some 200 barrels of tar were obtained. Furthermore, an expert in the making of naval stores declared that the white pines of New York, different from the pines of the Carolinas, were unfit for the industry. What made the whole affair even worse was that the Palatines, since they were mostly farmers and vineyard growers, were dissatisfied and particularly disliked working in gangs. They wanted their individual allotments of forty acres and a chance to farm them.

The project was a failure. In September 1712 Hunter, since he was still short of money, notified the Palatines that they would have to take care of themselves from then on. He advised them to seek work elsewhere in New York or New Jersey, though they would remain as the government's indentured servants until they had paid off their debts for the ocean passage and their subsistence in America.

Hunter's abandonment came as a rude surprise to the Palatines. Winter loomed ahead, and in desperation many scattered about the region, searching for work, although others remained in their original settlements. Several hundred decided their best chance was to go where they had first wanted to settle, in the Schoharie Valley. There, at least, if they could survive the winter, they could produce good crops to feed themselves. Governor Hunter issued an order forbidding them to move there, but they paid no attention to it.

Somehow most of the Palatines managed to get through the winter on the corn and other crops they had raised in their villages on the Hudson. In March 1713 those who had remained there joined the ones in the Schoharie Valley, except for some who wandered to New Jersey, Pennsylvania and New York City. That year was one of bitter struggle for the Schoharie settlers, although by 1714 they had almost as much corn as they needed. Meanwhile they eked out an existence with the help of friendly Mohawk Indians who told them about edible wild berries and roots, and through the charity of a number of kind people in Schenectady and New York City.

Men and women who made the round trip of about forty miles to Schenectady were able to obtain flour on credit. At the same time the Dutch church in New York sent corn, smoked pork, bread and £6 to

118

buy flour in Albany. The journey there and back took three or four days, but the Palatines were glad to make it.

Food was not their only problem. When spring came they had to plant crops, cultivate and in late summer harvest them. The New York authorities had acted to see that the Germans who defied their orders in moving from the Hudson River settlements took with them none of the tools with which they had been provided. But by ingenuity and hard work the Palatines made their own, presumably with a few axes, saws and knives they were able to spirit away.

For example, one made a shovel by hollowing out the end of a log. Another used tree branches to fashion a crude pitchfork. A sledge hammer or maul was made from a heavy knot of wood, with the branch for a handle. One man produced a mortar to grind corn by laboriously hollowing out one end of a log with his knife, making a hole a foot in diameter and about twenty inches deep. Many other makeshift tools and appliances were constructed with equal difficulty.

To furnish the log and mud huts they put up, the Palatines made rough furniture. They would split a big log, cut four holes in its outer side and fit in stout sticks of wood for the legs of a table. Smaller log sections were made into stools in the same way. It appears that at first the huts had no fireplaces and the people built stone ovens outdoors, each used by several families.

Sometimes they were able to make candles of the tallow from animals they killed or trapped; they doubtless used the early colonial method of twisting the silky down of milkweed pods into makeshift wicks and dipping them into the tallow time after time until a thick enough candle was formed. But most of the light they had came from pine knots, which burned with a smoky flame. As the clothes they had been furnished wore out, they fashioned new ones from deer and beaver skins. Moccasins were made from soft deerskin, and heavier shoes were fashioned from leather they tanned.

Meanwhile Governor Hunter had not given up. He ordered the Palatines to come back to the tracts near Livingston Manor to produce naval stores, but they refused. Hunter made no further move until 1715, when he ordered the Schoharie settlers either to buy or lease the Schoharie lands or get out. The Germans ignored the order and stayed.

Hunter was baffled. He decided to let the settlers stay for the time being. He could give the Board of Trade in London no encouraging word of any success that might repay the government for its costly investment in the Palatine naval stores venture. Rather lamely he reported one good result: the Schoharie settlers had strengthened the New York border. Although Queen Anne's War had ended, it was an uneasy truce, with the French in Canada still a threat, as well as their allies, the Canadian Algonquin tribes.

In 1717 Hunter told the Palatines he had received orders from England to move them to some other region. They refused. Then Hunter ordered them to do no plowing, hoping to starve them into submission, but they paid no attention.

In 1720 a new governor, William Burnet, inherited Hunter's troubles with the Palatines. He bought some land in the Mohawk Valley and ordered the Germans to move there. Few obeyed at first, but finally a few families did establish a settlement there. In 1723 a few more families, discouraged over being constantly harassed by the New York government, moved to Pennsylvania. Other groups appear to have followed them to this more hospitable and prosperous colony to the south.

So ended the British government's disastrous plan to use its own indentured servants to produce naval stores in New York. It must have taught the London authorities a lesson, for they indentured no more servants on their own account. They had learned it was better to let merchants and shipowners take care of obtaining them.

In general, German immigrants in America were trustful peasants and, as has been seen in the case of those who came to Pennsylvania, were easily victimized by the system of indentured servitude. Not all, however. One German who came over to New York as a redemptioner was indentured and served out his time. When given his freedom he showed his former master a good-sized bag of gold. The flabbergasted master asked why in the world the man had become an indentured servant with all that money. "Oh," was the reply, "I knew no English when I arrived and should have been cheated. Now I know all about the country and can set up for myself."

Nor were all indentured servants who came to New York badly treated. One unusual case was that of Elizabeth Morris, from England. The bark *Antigua,* in which she took passage, had been owned by Captain William Kidd before he became famous as a pirate. When Elizabeth reached New York, Kidd was living in the city and bought her as a house servant, indentured for four years.

Captain Kidd was a strange character. He followed the sea from boyhood and became so successful as a shipmaster that he finally settled down ashore in New York City. He bought a fine stone house in what is now downtown Manhattan and in 1691 married a widow, Sarah Ort Cox. There Kidd lived as a respected citizen; his occupation as given on his marriage certificate was "Gentleman."

It was during this time that Elizabeth Morris was his indentured house servant. But in 1696 the British government, anxious to stop the raiding of its merchant shipping by pirates, gave Kidd an armed ship in which to hunt them down as a privateer. But while he was roving the seas he decided to turn pirate himself and did so, accumulating much booty, part of which he is supposed to have buried on Gardiner's Island, just off the eastern tip of Long Island. Finally he was arrested and tried in London for piracy. He was convicted and hanged. A large store of gold and silver was found in his New York house.

But Elizabeth Morris seems to have had no complaint against the man who later became a notorious pirate. It appears that she was treated well and that Captain Kidd provided ample freedom dues when her time of servitude was up.

Although she was not the only indentured servant privately owned in New York, on the whole the colony showed less interest in the indenture system than did Pennsylvania and the southern colonies. Except for the ill-fated Palatine experiment in which they had no choice about where they would settle, Germans tended to avoid New York. Pennsylvania was their favorite place.

Nevertheless, New York would have preferred Germans to English and Irish. Particularly among the English immigrants, there were many paupers, beggars, convicts and servants who ran away. In 1721 New York attempted to stop the immigration of such servants with a law that required all incoming passengers to be registered. Captains of ships had to take undesirables back and could be fined £50 if any were allowed to land. However, the law was poorly enforced and New York continued to get riffraff who were not wanted.

Laws covering indentured servants in New York were much the same as in other colonies. Terms of indenture varied, but most commonly were about seven years for regular servants and five for redemptioners. The master's permission was required for servants to marry, those traveling any distance from the master's residence had to have passes, and they were forbidden to trade. Freedom dues varied. Sometimes they were liberal, but all the law had to say about this was that a freed servant should not be sent away "empty."

New York provided severe penalties for servants who misbehaved or ran away. Captured runaways usually had double the time they were absent added to their terms, as well as additional service to pay the cost of recovering them. Rewards to those who returned runaways to their masters averaged £5 if the runaways had been taken within the colony and £10 if outside it.

As in most other colonies, a servant who was abused by a master or not given enough food or clothing could bring his case before a justice of the peace. If the complaint was found justified, the master or mistress was required to post a bond to guarantee better treatment in the future. But if the judge found the complaint was not justified, as much as six months could be added to the servant's term of indenture. Unless the servant had good evidence to present or reliable witnesses, he would do well to consider the penalty before bringing his case to court.

All in all, New York was not an outstanding market for indentured servants. Many who emigrated did not have the abilities most needed in the colony and often had to take menial, unskilled work that gave them little chance of a good life when they were freed. And the complete failure of the naval stores project stands out as the greatest failure of the indentured-servant system in America.

While the Dutch still held New Netherland, which became the New York colony, New Jersey was virtually a part of it. Both colonies had the patroon system, and the Dutch government sent indentured servants to New Jersey as well.

Under English rule, New Jersey became a separate colony, but its indentured-servant system was much the same as New York's. New Jersey was more generous than some colonies, however, in granting land to indentured servants who had completed their servitude. The number of acres each servant received depended upon how long he had been in the colony and whether he was an adult or a child. Some got seventy-five acres, some fifty and others twenty-five.

Laws concerning indentured servants in New Jersey in regard to marriage, misbehavior, running away, complaints against masters and traveling alone were the same as in New York. But while New York said only that those who completed their terms should not be sent away empty, New Jersey laws required freedom dues of two suits of clothes, a good felling ax, a good hoe and seven bushels of Indian corn.

Indentured servants in New Jersey seem to have been well fed. A report in 1684 said they were given "beef, pork, bacon, pudding, milk and good beer and cider." Thus, on the whole, indentured servants in New Jersey seem to have been somewhat better off than in New York. But neither colony attracted as many as were needed, with the result that when black slavery commenced in America a fair number of African slaves were brought in.

10

HOW NEW ENGLAND HANDLED THE SERVANTS

There were 102 passengers aboard the *Mayflower* when she arrived in America on her famous voyage from Plymouth, England, in 1620. Her companion vessel, the *Speedwell*, developed such a bad leak that those aboard her had to be jammed into the *Mayflower*. One is apt to think of all in the ship as Pilgrims—Brownists and Separatists—who left England because of their religious disagreement with the Church of England. This is far from the truth. Although practically all adopted the Pilgrim way of life eventually, a good many of those who landed on Plymouth Rock were Anglicans, members of the Church of England, who made the voyage simply to find a better way of life in America. These outsiders were called "Strangers," while the true Pilgrims were known as "Saints."

Three of these Strangers became well known through Longfellow's famous but historically inaccurate poem, "The Courtship of Miles Standish." They were Myles (as he himself spelled it) Standish, a professional soldier; John Alden, the *Mayflower*'s cooper, who kept the barrels of beer, stronger spirits and water in the hold free of leaks during the voyage and decided to stay on in the American colony of Plymouth; and Priscilla Mullens, the teen-age girl who was later to marry John Alden. But the Strangers also included a group of indentured servants—eleven men, one woman and six children. They were the first indentured servants to come to New England.

The second recorded appearance of indentured servants there came in 1625 when a Captain Wollaston arrived aboard his ship in what is now Boston Bay. With him apparently were three well-to-do English adventurers, who brought along thirty or forty indentured servants. The new arrivals established a plantation, trading post and fishing station on the shore of the bay. The Indians called the place Passonagessit, but the settlement, on a hill, became known as Mount Wollaston.

Although almost nothing is known of Captain Wollaston, not even his first name, he seems to have been an honest and decent man. No more is known about his companion adventurers, with one exception. He was Thomas Morton, who called himself a "gentleman" but turned out to be a thorough rascal. The records of his past in England are scanty. Thomas Dudley, who later became governor of the Massachusetts Bay colony, wrote of Morton as a "proud, insolent man" and also intimated that he had been implicated in some serious crime in England. Another report had it that Morton had fled from England to escape a charge of murder.

The adventurers' choice of a site for their colony was not a very good one. The settlement itself stood on top of the hill with a fine view, but the country around it was either swampland near the shore or heavily forested ground broken only by a few small clearings where the Indians planted corn. Today it is within the city limits of Quincy, Massachusetts.

Thus it is not surprising that things did not go well at first for the new settlers. They built houses and cleared some land for a plantation, but Captain Wollaston, after undergoing his first bitter New England winter, had had enough. In the spring of 1626 he took some of the indentured servants and sailed to Virginia, where he sold the rest of their terms of servitude to planters at a good profit.

Wollaston then wrote one of his associates at Mount Wollaston to turn the government of the settlement over to another of the partners in the enterprise, take some more of the indentured servants and come to Virginia. This was done and these servants' unexpired terms were also sold to Virginia planters.

Seven servants, all with six years of servitude yet to be completed, remained at Mount Wollaston under the charge of the new head of the settlement, a man named Fitcher. Now Thomas Morton saw the chance for which he had been waiting. He plied the seven indentured servants with liquor until they were thoroughly drunk and then told them that if they would join him in overthrowing the settlement's head he would set them free at once. They agreed and mutinied against Fitcher, driving him to seek shelter at a nearby settlement. Morton then began to carry out the two purposes for which he had come to America—to enjoy himself and to make money.

To make money he used the Indians of the vicinity. The Indians, expert hunters and trappers, were glad to trade the valuable furs they obtained for goods the white men had to offer them—beads, cheap jewelry, mirrors, axes and other tools, blankets and the like.

What attracted them most, however, were firearms and liquor. In 1622 King James I of England had issued a proclamation forbidding the sale of firearms to American Indians. From the English point of view it was a wise precaution because the Indians, once armed with pistols, muskets and ammunition, would not have to rely on bows and arrows in warfare and could meet the white men on even terms. But unscrupulous white traders continued to sell firearms to the Indians and Thomas Morton, well out of reach of English law, cared not a fig for the king's order.

Morton also supplied the Indians around Mount

Wollaston with plenty of "firewater," as the Indians called liquor. There was no English order or law forbidding its sale to them, but colony governments frowned on it. Drunken quarrels among the Indians could lead to violence against the colonists.

Piles of bear, otter, marten, wolf and beaver furs and deerskins mounted high in Morton's storehouse and he grew rich. He could now enjoy himself and he did. He roamed the countryside with his fowling piece, shooting wildfowl as delicacies for his table, and explored the coast in his sailboat. To show what a joyous place Mount Wollaston was, he renamed it Merry-Mount. When the spring of 1627 came, great preparations were afoot for a gala celebration of May Day.

In England, May Day had long been a time for revelry, and Morton was determined that Merry-Mount should observe the custom. He had a Maypole erected and the settlers, along with Indian guests from miles around, took part in dancing around the pole, playing games, feasting and drinking.

Word of all this soon reached Plymouth, about twenty miles to the south, where Thomas Morton was well and unfavorably known. The Pilgrim minister and the elders of the church were shocked and alarmed. May Day merrymaking was sinful in their eyes, and liquor consumed by the Indians a real menace. Dancing was a forbidden pastime—and dancing around that contraption of the Devil, a Maypole, worst of all. They warned Morton to stop such orgies at once. He sent an insolent reply to the message.

In May 1628 the Pilgrims took action. They sent Myles Standish, the colony's military commander, with eight men to arrest Thomas Morton. When Standish arrived, Morton foxily changed his tune. He explained that he was minding his own business and doing no harm with his simple amusements. Why should he be persecuted in this way?

His innocent guise did not help him. Standish seized him and put him under guard of six men, but that night all six fell asleep and Morton escaped. He disappeared into the forest, and while Standish and his men were searching for him, he returned to Merry-Mount and prepared to defend himself. To aid him he had only the seven formerly indentured servants, and of these, five were away, probably looking for furs. So when Standish learned that Morton was back, he marched on Merry-Mount. Morton made a brief show of resistance, but it was hopeless. The Pilgrims tore down the hated Maypole, seized Morton and took him to Plymouth, where he was shipped back to England.

Exactly what happened to the indentured servants Morton had freed is not known except that several remained at Merry-Mount, which was no longer the gay place it had been, and others wandered away.

They probably made their own ways as freemen.

Save for their brief spree with the knavish Morton, the lot of these men was probably not a particularly pleasant one. In fact, New England in general was not a favorite destination for indentured servants. As settlement in America increased and the indentured-servant and redemptioner systems came into full swing in the colonies, New England was the least attractive market for the sale of these servants.

For one thing, there appears to have been some opposition there to the system. Black slavery was disliked, although there were some African slaves in New England, and the idea of white slavery seems to have been even more offensive to many New Englanders.

Another reason was that New England was largely a region of small farms. It was rare that a New England family had more than one indentured servant, while many shunned them completely. During colonial days only a few shiploads of indentured servants arrived in New England. However, quite a number of Scots, prisoners and rebels, were sent to Massachusetts after a rebellion was crushed in Dundee, Scotland.

Irish indentured servants were especially unpopular. New England was thoroughly Protestant, and its colonists had brought with them from England a deep-seated dislike and even hatred of Roman Catholics. In 1718 and 1719 some Irish who arrived in

New England were given a cold welcome. A few
Irish immigrants made themselves well liked, but
for the most part New England had no use for them.
In fact, Boston, today a city with a very large Irish
population, took measures to keep them out in the
eighteenth century. There are two records in Boston
dated November 7, 1737, showing indemnities paid
to the town for importing Irish servants. One was a
bond of £600; the other, £1,000. Such a high bond
for the good behavior of Irish servants would hardly
be paid unless some rich man was especially anxious
to have them. In 1777 seven Irishmen who arrived
and could find no one to put up the bonds required
for them were banished from Boston.

Rhode Island, famous for its liberality in allowing
religious freedom for all, nevertheless tried to keep
out not only Irish but English indentured servants.
In 1729 it required captains of ships bringing passengers from England or Ireland to post a bond of
£50 for each one. It would appear, however, that
this was due more to dislike of slavery than religious
intolerance.

The laws of Massachusetts regarding freedom
dues, like those of New York, contained only the
vague promise that freed servants, after seven years,
"must not be sent away empty." The phrase probably originated in Puritan Massachusetts Bay, where
obedience to the laws set forth in the Old Testament
was strictly followed. In Chapter 15 of the Book of

Deuteronomy is the following: "And if thy brother, an Hebrew man or an Hebrew woman, be sold unto thee, and serve thee six years, then in the seventh year thou shalt let him go free from thee. And when thou sendest him out free from thee, thou shalt not let him go away empty." This also shows that something like the indentured-servant system was nothing new in the world.

John Hunting of Dedham, Massachusetts, decided to send his maidservant, Abigail Littlefield, away empty by letting the town see to her later welfare when she had served out her term and was unable to support herself. When Hunting bought Abigail, she must have been either old or in poor health, for the Dedham selectmen sternly reminded him that he had taken her against both their advice and their orders. Therefore, they said, he ought to be able to support her himself. However, they did grant him £4 to continue her support for another year.

When the year elapsed, Hunting apparently proposed to send Abigail out to shift for herself. She appeared before the selectmen to complain against it, saying she was "under a great affliction by extraordinary burning." The town gave Hunting 24 shillings to pay for a cure of her ailment and £5 to help support her for another year. The records do not say whether poor Abigail died or was turned out when the second year ended.

Other New England masters were no more gener-

ous with freedom dues. In Charlestown, Massachusetts, Margery Bateman, indentured for four years,
was rewarded only with one she-goat when her term
ended.

There are few reports about punishments in New
England, although two harsh instances are recorded.
The first was described briefly in the journal kept by
John Winthrop, who was four times governor of
Massachusetts Bay in the first half of the seventeenth
century. Winthrop told of a boy indentured to a
master who treated him badly. The boy became un-
ruly and his master beat him unmercifully. As a result the boy died and the master was hanged.

The second instance concerns a master in Essex
County, Massachusetts, who punished his indentured servant severely for some offense which is not
recorded. Mistreated servants could bring complaints to court, and this unnamed one did, charging
that he had been "hung up by the heels as butchers
do to beasts for the slaughter." In this case the court
merely rebuked the cruel master mildly. Nevertheless, in New England as in other northern colonies, a
master who maimed a servant could be forced to free
him and also provide for his support and cure.
There appear to be no records in New England to
show that such justice was ever done.

It was not easy for freed indentured servants to
get along in New England. Society there tended to
look down on them as of low class. Since most of

them worked on small farms, about the best a freed servant, if a man, could hope for was to continue working for whatever wages he could get as a "hired man"; a woman, unless she married, could usually depend only on housework to support herself.

Generally, New England was no place for an ambitious immigrant, yet there were exceptions. A seven-year-old boy was sold to a master in Windsor, Connecticut, to serve until he was twenty-one, but his indenture provided that his master was to teach him to read and write. The boy evidently had a scalp ailment, for it was also provided that the master was to "get his scurf [an old word meaning either dandruff or scaliness] head cured." Moreover, since the master was a cooper, the boy would learn the trade of making and repairing barrels and casks, a good trade to know in those days when Connecticut River settlements shipped out a good deal of tobacco in hogsheads.

What brightens the rather dismal account of indentured servants in New England most, however, is the charming story of Elizabeth Hanley. In the early years of the eighteenth century, Elizabeth, who lived in western England, was attending what the English call a public, and Americans a private, school; thus it would appear that her father was well off. Elizabeth was eighteen and about to finish her education.

In those days a girl's parents would often choose a husband for her. Elizabeth received a letter from her father one day saying, "You will soon be at home for good, and as all girls should be thinking of a home of their own, and as a good husband, who is able to provide well for you, I have promised your hand in marriage to a brother of my best friend—although older than yourself, he will make an excellent husband. So prepare your mind for this event."

Elizabeth Hanley had a mind of her own. She wanted no husband who was chosen for her, especially an older man and one she had never even met. She went to nearby Liverpool, the great seaport from which many ships departed for America. A vessel was preparing to sail for the little Connecticut River port of Pettipaug (today Essex, Connecticut). Elizabeth went aboard and talked with the captain, telling him she had no money but was sure she could find work in America and pay him later for her passage. He agreed to take her as a passenger.

Several weeks later the ship arrived at Pettipaug. That same morning Joshua Bushnell, Jr., a young man from nearby Saybrook, had started out for Pettipaug driving a yoke of oxen. His father had asked him to sell the two animals there. The young man was at the wharf when Elizabeth's ship warped in there. Joshua thought he could probably sell the oxen to the captain as part of his return cargo.

Then he saw Elizabeth on the wharf, alone, frightened and not knowing what she should do next. She was a pretty girl and Joshua was instantly taken with her. When he heard her story he traded the oxen to the captain in exchange for Elizabeth's passage money.

Back in Saybrook, Elizabeth served on the Bushnell farm as an indentured servant until she had repaid the passage money. Then, on February 23, 1717, Joshua Bushnell, Jr., and Elizabeth Hanley were married—a happy ending to the love story of a courageous English girl and a young Connecticut farmer. They were members of a family whose name was to become famous in the Revolution when David Bushnell of Saybrook built the *Turtle*, believed to be the first really practical submarine. The *Turtle* came very close to sinking a big British man-of-war in New York harbor during the war.

The records appear to be silent about the last of the New England colonies, New Hampshire. It is plain that this colony's indentured servants, if any, were very few in number.

Altogether, New England had the fewest indentured servants and made no real effort to obtain them, since there was comparatively little demand for them.

11

THE SOLDIERS AND
PETER FRANCISCO

The period in which the system of indentured servants flourished in America was also a time of continual warfare. Between 1689 and 1760 the colonies, particularly the northern ones, were torn by successive colonial wars fought by both English and American forces against the French in Canada and the Spanish in Florida—King William's War from 1689 to 1697; Queen Anne's War, 1702 to 1713; the combined war, first against Spain and then against France, 1739 to 1748; and the French and Indian War, 1755 to 1760.

Indentured servants were enlisted along with free colonists for service in these wars; in fact, some servants took part in the earlier Indian wars in New England. In the first three colonial conflicts, a good many of the fighting men came from New England, since it, as well as New York to some extent, was in the greatest danger of invasion from Canada.

During Queen Anne's War, Pennsylvania was in no great peril and the colony's government com-

plained in 1711 about the efforts of British recruiting officers to enlist the indentured servants. It
claimed the queen herself should pay their masters
for the labor lost as a result. It even kept money it
had granted as a gift to the queen in order to repay
the masters, although there is no record that this was
ever done.

An English war against Spain spread to the colonies in 1740, where it was fought against the Spaniards in Florida and the French in Canada. In the
colonies it was called King George's War. British recruiters then resumed their efforts to persuade indentured servants to enlist. In this war, too, Pennsylvania was not seriously endangered, but about 300
Pennsylvania servants were induced to enlist, and
their masters again set up a great outcry.

There was a long struggle between Pennsylvania's
governor, who believed the servants had a right to
enlist, and the colony's assembly, which opposed it.
But finally the assembly did vote £2,589 to be paid
to the masters of the 300 enlisted servant-soldiers.

In the French and Indian War Pennsylvania was
seriously threatened by the French who held Fort
Duquesne in the far western part of that colony, and
Maryland and Virginia were also alarmed. Yet when
British General Braddock's expedition against Duquesne was nearly annihilated in 1755 and fear
spread that the French and their Indians would
strike westward, the greed of indentured servants'

masters was greater than their fear. They resisted the attempts of recruiting officers to enlist their servants for defense of the three colonies, demanding compensation for the loss of their labor while serving in the war.

When word of the Pennsylvania resistance reached Parliament in England, the members decided that if any master objected to the enlistment of one of his servants, the servant should either be returned to him or the master paid an amount of money to be determined by the local justices of the peace. The owners of indentured servants in Pennsylvania promptly handed in a list of 680 who had enlisted. The Earl of Loudon, then in command of all troops fighting in America, refused to use crown funds to pay the large sum that would be needed. In the end the Pennsylvania Assembly appears to have voted money for this purpose.

Since Maryland and Virginia were also threatened by French invasion from the west during the French and Indian War, indentured servants were enlisted in those colonies and there was a similar uproar from their masters. Resistance to enlistment was particularly strong in Maryland, probably because most masters there lived in the eastern part of the colony and felt safer from invasion. The colony records do not show how much was paid masters there for the loss of services, but they were compensated to some extent. In Virginia the governor introduced a plan that would put a value on each servant who enlisted, according to the kind of work he did.

During the American Revolution, the inducement for indentured servants to enlist was quite different. In the colonial wars both British and American forces had been fighting common enemies. But servants who enlisted during the Revolution could choose whether to fight for Britain or the colonies.

British recruiting officers were quick to take advantage of dissatisfaction among indentured servants. Those who had been ill-treated were more easily persuaded to join the British side. And runaways, always in danger of being captured and returned to their masters for possible brutal punishment and almost certain extension of their terms of servitude, often chose to fight against the colonists. The British even offered special inducements to prospective recruits who were serving under indentures.

On the other hand, some indentured servants had no cause to complain against their masters, loved America, favored the colonies in their struggle for freedom and enlisted on the American side. Others joined because they felt that military service, regardless of its danger, would be better than their present condition. Probably some saw it as an exciting ad-

venture and a relief from the monotony and hardship of toiling in plantation fields or sweating to
clear forested land.

Just as in the colonial wars, masters set up an out-
raged howl over the loss of indentured servants'
labor due to enlistment. In Pennsylvania the Council of Safety passed a resolution forbidding indentured servants to enlist without the written permission of their masters. Some servants went ahead and
enlisted without it, however, and in 1778 the council
passed a law to compensate owners who lost indentured servants to the American armies.

For a short time Virginia strongly backed enlistment by indentured servants and by black slaves—
but only on the British side. In 1775 the colony's
governor, the Earl of Dunmore, promised freedom
to both white servants and black slaves who enlisted
to fight the Americans. Soon afterward patriots
forced the governor to flee for his life to safety
aboard a British warship.

The majority of indentured servants did not enlist on either side, however. They believed that regardless of whether Britain or America won they
probably would be returned to their masters, perhaps punished and surely have their terms of servitude extended. It would be better, they thought, to
serve out their terms and be free.

One vengeful enlistment was that of Johann Karl
Buettner. The story of how he was lured into mak-

ing an unwanted voyage to America is told in Chapter 3, up to his arrival in Philadelphia, where he was sold as an indentured servant. His owner had a plantation across the Delaware River in New Jersey. Johann was treated so brutally that he persuaded some other German servants on the plantation to join him in an attempt to run away.

They must have thought they were perfectly safe when they had traveled three hundred miles and had reached Virginia, but fate was against them. Someone became suspicious of a group of Germans wandering about the countryside and they were seized and returned to New Jersey, where they were punished severely.

When the Revolution began, Johann, having no love for America, decided to enlist on the British side in some Hessian regiment. But the opportunity did not come and Johann, feeling that anything would be better than the agonies of his servitude, joined the American army.

Johann was captured, perhaps not against his will, by the British. His captors soon found out that he favored their side and took him before their commanding general, Earl Cornwallis. After Cornwallis had interviewed him, he offered him service in a Hessian regiment. Johann accepted eagerly and fought the rest of the Revolution with the Hessians and no doubt vented his spite against his American master during the fighting in which he took part.

However, one indentured servant on the American side stands out not only for his patriotism but because as a fighting man he had no rival among other American enlisted men. He was Peter Francisco, and his story is a thrilling and unusual one.

In about the year 1765 a ship arrived off City Point (today Hopewell), Virginia, and anchored. A small boat with a child in it was lowered away and rowed by several sailors to the wharf. The oarsmen left the child there and returned to the ship, which then sailed away.

Those who found the little boy on the wharf were puzzled. He was about five or six years old, dressed in rich clothing with the fine lace collar and cuffs worn by gentlemen of quality at that time, and his shoes were fastened with large silver buckles bearing the initials P. F. When he spoke, it was in a mixture of Spanish and Portuguese, together with a few words of English he had apparently picked up during the voyage.

Someone who knew a little Spanish questioned the child and learned that the ship's captain had persecuted him and the crew had become convinced he was a "Jonah," the seafaring man's term for an omen of ill fortune. Perhaps that was why the boy had been abandoned at City Point. He told his questioner that his name was Peter Francisco.

Peter did not seem to know how he had gotten aboard the ship, but it appeared that he had been kidnaped. Peter thought he came either from Spain or Portugal, but was not sure which. There is a story that in the eighteenth century a boy of the high-ranking house of Francisco in Spain was ordered beheaded because of his father's political activities, but the child disappeared before the execution could be carried out. Perhaps Peter was that child, sent to America alone to escape his father's enemies. However, in America, Peter was considered to be of Portuguese extraction.

The parish authorities in City Point took charge of the boy. He had such fine manners and such a frank and courageous way about him that they had no trouble in placing him as an indentured servant on the estate of Anthony Winston, an uncle of the famous Patrick Henry, at Hunting Tower, Buckingham County, in central Virginia.

In spite of his youth, Peter was a good worker, for even at that age his strength was so great that it was a marvel of the countryside. Moreover, his master soon felt full confidence in him because of his honesty and frankness and gave him responsibilities that ordinarily would have fallen to an intelligent adult. Peter became well acquainted with and respected by Patrick Henry, who was often a visitor at Hunting Tower.

After the Revolution began, Peter Francisco enlisted on the American side as soon as possible. He was too young in 1775, but in the fall of 1776, when he was about sixteen, he joined the Continental Army as one of the 10th Virginia Regiment. It was the beginning of Peter's spectacular career as an American soldier.

He was then a young giant, six feet six inches tall and weighing 260 pounds. His strength was prodigious, and he came early to the attention of General Washington.

When an ordinary sword issued to Peter was too short and light for him to use with the devastating effect on the enemy of which he was capable, the general ordered a special one made for him in the camp's blacksmith shop. It was five feet long, yet young Peter handled it as if it had been a feather.

Washington offered Peter Francisco an officer's commission, but the young man refused because he felt he did not have enough education. For three years he used his tremendous strength and fighting genius effectively in many battles and skirmishes. He was at Brandywine, where he was wounded, at Germantown and Monmouth.

In 1779 Peter's regiment, under command of Brigadier General "Mad Anthony" Wayne, took part in the storming and capture of Stony Point on the Hudson River in New York. To accomplish what seemed an impossibility, Wayne sent two columns of troops against the strategic British-held fort from separate directions. Preceding each column were "forlorn hope" units of twenty men each. In military language a forlorn hope is a group of soldiers used in such a desperate situation that their chances of survival are poor. Peter Francisco was one of these presumably doomed men who were being sacrificed in order to wipe out sentinels who could give the alarm of the attack. In the rush on Stony Point he received a nine-inch bayonet wound across his stomach, but he plunged on and was the second man to enter the fort.

Peter Francisco's enlistment expired, but not his fighting career. He went back to Virginia and re-enlisted in a militia regiment that fought in the crucial southern campaign. He was in the battle of Camden, South Carolina, in which the Americans suffered a disastrous defeat largely because of the incompetence of Major General Horatio Gates. After the rout at Camden, Gates deserted the remainder of his troops and rode at full speed for 180 miles before he felt safe from the British.

But Peter Francisco distinguished himself in this battle. While it was in progress the horses used to haul the American artillery were shot dead. When a cannon was needed in another part of the battlefield, Peter is said to have wrestled a gun weighing 1,000 pounds to the place where it was wanted. After the battle Peter's commanding officer, Colonel William Mayo, was captured by a British grenadier. The enemy soldier was about to run Mayo through with his sword when Peter sent a bullet crashing into the redcoat's skull and Mayo was saved.

Francisco was a hero in another decisive battle. Major General Nathanael Greene, second only to Washington among the great generals of the Revolution, lured British General Cornwallis into pursuing him and his American army through South and North Carolina to the Virginia border in one of the most successful retreats in military history. When Cornwallis was too far from his nearest base of supplies to obtain food and equipment for his army, he was forced to meet Greene at Guilford Courthouse, North Carolina. The British won, but their victory was as hollow as that at Bunker Hill. The battle resulted in a long, hardship-ridden British retreat that finally ended with Cornwallis's surrender at Yorktown.

Peter Francisco was then in the cavalry under the command of Washington's relative, Colonel William Washington. On that day at Guilford Courthouse—March 15, 1781—Peter is said to have killed eleven redcoats with his mighty broadsword until, in a cavalry charge, he received a severe bayonet wound and fell among a pile of dead bodies. After the battle he was rescued by a Quaker and recovered from his wound.

Later, while still with the American army in the south, Peter one day was in a tavern in Virginia kept by Benjamin Ward. Suddenly the place was surrounded by British cavalry. Those in the tavern were petrified with fear, but Francisco, unarmed, stepped outside. Two riders galloped up to him, one demanding his watch and the other his silver knee buckles. While Peter pretended he would comply, the cavalrymen dismounted. As one stopped to take the buckles off, he placed his sword under one arm. In a flash, Peter stepped back a pace, seized the man's sword and cut his head off.

Just then a body of British cavalry appeared in the distance. Peter recognized them instantly by their green coats as part of Colonel Banastre Tarleton's force, known as the Green Dragoons.

Tarleton was probably the most feared and hated British officer in the south during the campaign. A cruel, merciless man, he was himself known as the Green Dragoon. With his men he roamed the countryside, swooping down on American detachments or springing at them from ambush, often butchering them all; in one case he did so after an American party had surrendered.

Peter Francisco's mind was as agile as his body was powerful. He began to shout orders as if speaking to a large force of American troops inside the tavern. Tarleton, drawing nearer, decided the enemy must be too strong for him and ordered his dragoons to withdraw.

Peter leaped into the saddle of one of the horses

from which the two cavalrymen had dismounted before Tarleton's approach, and escaped down a side road, driving the other animal before him. Realizing that he had been tricked, Tarleton sent his men searching in all directions, but Peter eluded them. He kept one of the horses and named him Tarleton.

Peter took part in the final siege of the war at Yorktown. There he served under the great French general, the Marquis de Lafayette, whom he had met earlier. When the war was over Peter kept a tavern in Virginia for some years; taught himself to read, though he could never write; became sergeant-at-arms, appointed to keep order in the Virginia House of Delegates; and was welcomed among the best groups of society in Virginia until his death in 1831.

This former indentured servant left behind him a shining mark for valor in action. If his feats of heroism had taken place in the nineteenth or twentieth centuries, Peter Francisco would doubtless have been one of the select group of American military and naval heroes to receive the government's highest decoration, the Congressional Medal of Honor.

12

OTHERS WHO MADE GOOD

Peter Francisco was not the only indentured servant who attained success in life. Just how many cannot be estimated, of course. But certainly many thousands were successful in their occupations and made good and useful citizens. A number of former indentured servants reached high places in government, industry and trade. Others had families or descendants who became notable. Benjamin Franklin, probably the wisest man in colonial America and the early days of the republic, was the grandson of an indentured woman servant.

The story of the German and German-speaking Swiss people in Pennsylvania is one of which their descendants may be proud. In spite of all their hardships in reaching America and working out their indentures, they made the Pennsylvania Dutch country the prosperous agricultural region it still is today and contributed much to Pennsylvania's industrial importance.

Of the indentured servants who came with the

Pilgrims to Plymouth in the *Mayflower*, John Howland rose highest in later life. He was the servant of a merchant named John Carver. Carver seems to have been quite well off, although he could not be called a "gentleman" of the upper class in England because everyone aboard the ship had been of the lower class. While working in the fields that first summer of 1621, Carver was stricken with sunstroke and died. Mrs. Carver died soon afterward, "of a broken heart" according to the records, and there were no children. The estate went to John Howland, who must have been highly regarded by the Carvers.

This was a piece of good fortune for John Howland, but he was not content simply to take the money and property and live in greater comfort than the rest of the *Mayflower*'s indentured servants. He bought his freedom and in about 1624 was married to Elizabeth Tilley, one of the Saints. During their lifetime they had nine children.

By 1627 Howland had become influential enough to become an "undertaker"—not a funeral director, as the word is used today, but one of those in charge of trading in the colony. The records are not clear, but probably from 1629 to 1633 he was assistant governor of the Plymouth colony; it is definitely known that he occupied that position from 1633 to 1635.

Howland might have risen even higher but for an

unfortunate occurrence. The Plymouth colonists were great traders. As an undertaker, Howland was among those who established trading posts along the Kennebec and Penobscot rivers of present-day Maine.

One day in 1634 while he was at the Kennebec trading post, a bark from New Hampshire sailed up the river. Her captain, a man named Hocking, announced that he and his ship's company intended to build a trading post farther up the Kennebec. This would enable New Hampshire traders to intercept the furs the Indians brought down the river to exchange for the usual trinkets, tools, blankets and other merchandise and would cut off the Pilgrims' profitable business.

John Alden was also at the Pilgrim post on the Kennebec. He and Howland decided that Hocking and his men must be prevented from carrying out their venture. At first they tried persuasion but got only abuse for their pains. So a canoe with two men in it was sent out to cut the bark's anchor cables; thus the intruders would be unable to anchor farther up the river and would have to return to New Hampshire.

The cables were cut, and as the bark swung about in the river current, Hocking went to the rail and shot and killed one of the men in the canoe. The other boatman seized a musket and shot Hocking dead.

A number of ugly and untrue rumors sprang up concerning what had happened. The Massachusetts Bay colony began an investigation. Massachusetts Bay was not then particularly friendly to Plymouth and the results of its inquiry blamed the Pilgrims as well as Hocking. When John Alden, returning to Plymouth by sea, was forced by bad weather to put into Boston, the Massachusetts Bay authorities had him arrested for murder and threw him into jail, though he was later released.

John Howland was also innocent of Hocking's murder, but a certain amount of blame for the incident fell upon him in Plymouth, and after his term as assistant governor expired, he was never again given any public office in the colony. This, in contrast to his inheritance, was purely bad luck, but it cannot take away credit to John Howland as the most successful of the indentured servants aboard the *Mayflower*.

Perhaps the most famous of the men and women who had been indentured servants was Matthew Thornton. His parents, James and Elizabeth Thornton, of Scotch-Irish origin, came to America in about 1718, bringing with them their son, Matthew, who was probably four or five years old. The family settled as indentured servants in Maine, then still part of the Massachusetts Bay colony.

After working out their terms of servitude, the

Thorntons moved to Worcester, Massachusetts. There Matthew received his early education. He then began to study medicine, and in 1740, at about twenty-six, he went to Londonderry, New Hampshire, to practice as a doctor.

A few years later his work was interrupted, however. During King George's War the French threatened New England from a mighty stronghold, the fortress of Louisbourg on the tip of Cape Breton Island, just off the eastern end of Nova Scotia. The French believed no one could capture it, and so did most American colonists. But one man, William Pepperrell, a merchant of Kittery, Maine, with little military experience, thought he could do it. He assembled a motley group of farmers and fishermen and sailed for Louisbourg. Doctor Thornton volunteered to go along as a surgeon.

Pepperrell accomplished the incredible feat of capturing Louisbourg in 1745. Thornton shared in the glory and was commissioned as colonel in the Massachusetts Bay militia. However, from then on, his career was largely in politics and government.

He continued to live in Londonderry, married and had five children. In 1758 he was elected to the New Hampshire legislature and for thirty years was a leader in New Hampshire politics.

Before the Revolution, Matthew Thornton became an ardent patriot, especially in the resistance against the Stamp Act. The act, passed by the British Parliament in 1765, levied taxes on every sort of document and newspaper in the American colonies. As the clouds of armed revolution grew darker, Thornton became chairman of the New Hampshire Committee of Safety, one of the secret groups formed in the colonies to prepare for war. He was also elected president of the New Hampshire Provincial Congress in 1775.

When the Revolution broke out, Thornton was chosen president of New Hampshire's constitutional convention. New Hampshire was the first American colony to draw up a constitution, and it was from this beginning that the Constitution of the United States came into being after the Revolution was won.

The New Hampshire group drew up its constitution in December 1775 and January 1776. Matthew Thornton knew what it was to be an indentured servant, deprived of a freeman's rights. He must have used his influence as much as possible to persuade the convention that the people should vote on whether the new constitution should be accepted. Of all the colonies, only New Hampshire and Massachusetts submitted their constitutions to the people for approval.

The Declaration of Independence was first published in Philadelphia on July 4, 1776, and on August 2 a copy written in script on parchment was

signed by fifty-three delegates to the Continental
Congress. At that time Matthew Thornton was
speaker of the New Hampshire House of Representatives. In 1777 he was elected to the Continental
Congress and was among the three new members
who were allowed to add their signatures to the Declaration. A glance at a copy of the great document
shows Matthew Thornton's name squeezed into the
lower right-hand corner.

Thus Matthew Thornton, who as a boy had
been a white slave, became one of the famous signers
of the Declaration. He continued to be active in the
New Hampshire government until he died in 1803.

Another man who had been an indentured servant also became mighty in the affairs of our country. Matthew Lyon was a very different type of person from Matthew Thornton. He was a tough,
pugnacious, red-haired Irishman, born in County
Wicklow, Ireland, in 1750. He decided to go to
America when he was about fifteen. Unlike most
Irish immigrants, who generally were not welcome
in New England, Matthew Lyon came to Connecticut. He was sold to Jabez Bacon of Woodbury for
three years of servitude to work out the cost of his
translatlantic passage.

Once Lyon was free he managed to make a living
for himself and married a Miss Hosford of nearby
Litchfield. She was a cousin of Ethan Allen, who was
destined to become famous as the leader of the

Green Mountain Boys in the New Hampshire Grants, now Vermont. Matthew Lyon must have been acquainted with Allen in western Connecticut, for Allen came from the same region and, although at that time he had already settled on the Grants, he often came back on visits to his old home.

In 1771 Lyon bought land in Wallingford in to-day's western Vermont and moved there. Ethan Allen and his mob of Green Mountain Boys, tough, brawling, hard-drinking farmers, were then carrying on a war with the "Yorkers." The New York colony disputed the ownership of the Grants with New Hampshire, and New York land speculators were trying to drive out settlers who had bought their land from New Hampshire.

Ethan Allen was Matthew Lyon's kind of man. Like Matthew, he was big and rough. He had a thunderous voice and was a boastful man. Although he was really no military expert, he and his "army" of Green Mountain Boys were making life miserable for the New York speculators, accompanied by sheriffs' posses, who were trying to evict the Grants settlers from their land. Matthew Lyon joined the Green Mountain Boys.

Then along came the Revolution. The "Yorker" war was forgotten and Ethan and his mob turned their attention to a great idea their leader had.

Things were looking bad for the ragged, un-trained and undisciplined men who flocked to Cambridge, outside Boston, immediately after the Revolution began. They had no uniforms and few muskets, fewer cannon and little enough ammunition. Not many people thought they had any chance against Britain's military power. British General John Burgoyne called them a "rabble in arms" and he was right at that time. But Ethan Allen thought he could put heart into American patriots by capturing the British-held fortress of Ticonderoga.

Just as had been the case with Louisbourg in 1745, "Ti," as people called it, was supposed to be mighty indeed, although there were woods rangers like Ethan Allen who had been in the vicinity and thought differently of the old, neglected fort. Nevertheless, a good many people thought Allen was crazy to think famous Ti could be captured.

But Allen and the Green Mountain Boys crossed Lake Champlain to where Ticonderoga stood on the west bank, swooped down at dawn on May 10, 1775, and seized the fort. Matthew Lyon was with them in that famous attack. It did not matter that the woods rangers were right, that the British had let Ticonderoga begin to fall into ruin or that it was manned only by two low-ranking officers and a handful of rather decrepit redcoats. The Green Mountain Boys' feat put new heart into the American colonies in their struggle for freedom. And in the dead of that next winter a brave band of Americans suffered great hardships and difficulties in dragging Ticonderoga's big cannon across the mountains to the Continental Army's fortifications outside Boston. It was those big guns that enabled the Americans to drive the British out of Boston.

So no doubt Matthew Lyon joined with the other Green Mountain Boys that May morning when, after discovering the fort's stock of liquor, they "tossed around the flowing bowl and wished success to Congress and the liberty and freedom of America," as Ethan Allen himself described it. In fact, a story is told of how Lyon decided something special ought to be done to celebrate the victory. Among the big guns at Ticonderoga was an enormous thirteen-inch mortar known as the "Old Sow." Lyon went into the fort's magazine, filled a bucket brimful of powder, poured it down the Old Sow's gaping muzzle and touched off the charge. It was said that the blast seemed to rock the fort itself and the roar was so tremendous that it roused several Green Mountain Boys who were in a drunken stupor after too much of the "flowing bowl."

Lyon went on fighting for freedom. When Brigadier General Richard Montgomery marched north into Canada in December 1775 and barely failed to capture the fortress city of Quebec from the British, Matthew Lyon was with his force. In 1777 he was with the American army in Canada that failed to keep General Burgoyne and his big British army from invading the colonies by way of Lake Champlain, and back at Ticonderoga again with Major General Arthur St. Clair when Burgoyne recaptured the fort. Then Lyon fought with distinction in the military operations that led to the great American victory at Saratoga in 1777, when Burgoyne was forced to surrender his entire army and the tide of the Revolution turned for the first time toward American victory.

Matthew Lyon's active fighting in the Revolution ended then and his career in politics began when he was elected to the Vermont legislature and also served as secretary to the governor and his council. Then for some years Lyon left politics. He settled in Fair Haven, Vermont, in 1783 and became one of the leading businessmen of Vermont, which was a small independent republic until it joined the Union as a state in 1791. In Fair Haven Lyon operated iron works, manufactured paper, ran a printing press and cut and shipped timber through Lake Champlain and on to Montreal.

Matthew Lyon could not keep out of politics, however, and in 1796 he was elected a congressman from Vermont. He was always a radical and in Congress bitterly opposed the aristocratic Federalist party. His experience as an indentured servant made him a strong supporter of freedom and the rights of the common people.

Lyon got himself into trouble over the Sedition Act, passed by Congress in 1798. Among other things, the act prohibited the publishing of anything designed to bring public contempt or a bad reputation upon the government, Congress or the President. Lyon believed it would interfere with freedom of speech and of the press, two of the most important liberties the United States has always had. He denounced the Federalists who supported the passage of the Sedition Act, including President John Adams.

Lyon's enemies had him prosecuted for this, claiming his outbursts violated the Sedition Act. He was tried, fined $1,000 and served four months in the cheerless jail in Vergennes, Vermont. But he came bouncing back, ready to take up the fight again. The story of his imprisonment had spread all over the country and he became a hero to the people. When he ran in Vermont for re-election to Congress he won by an overwhelming majority. He went back to the capital, then in Philadelphia, in a triumphal procession. Matthew Lyon did not live to see his vindication, but in 1840 the fine he had paid was refunded to his heirs.

The rest of his life continued to be stormy in politics. He moved to Kentucky and was elected to Congress from that state, continuing his fight for the rights of the people. In 1820 his friend, President James Monroe, sent him to Arkansas as the factor or government overseer of the Cherokee Indian nation on the reservation there. Since Arkansas had not yet become a state and Lyon could not be a congressman again, he ran for the office of territorial delegate to Congress and was elected, but he died in 1822 before he could take his seat in Washington.

Here was a one-time indentured servant who never forgot his enslavement and spent the greater part of his life fighting for American freedoms.

Another indentured servant who left a distinguished record of public service to his country was Charles Thomson. He was born in Maghera, County Derry, Ireland, in 1729. When he was ten his parents sailed from the impoverished and stricken island to make a new life for themselves and their six children in America. Either because of their weakened condition when they sailed or the hardships they endured on the voyage, both parents died aboard the ship. Charles and the other five orphaned children were sold as indentured servants when they landed at New Castle, Delaware.

Charles was a smart and ambitious boy. When he had served out his term he was able to enter an academy in New London, Chester County, Pennsylvania. He proved to be a brilliant student, and when he finished his education he established a private school of his own. While he was in Pennsylvania he met and became a lifelong friend of Benjamin Franklin, who realized the young man's abilities and used his influence to have Thomson appointed a tutor in the Philadelphia Academy. From there he went as headmaster to the Latin School, which became the William Penn Charter School, whose reputation for the high quality of its instruction eventually made it the largest preparatory school for boys in the United States.

Charles Thomson was a completely honest man. His reputation for integrity became known not only to the authorities of the American colonies but to the Indians of Pennsylvania. In 1758 the Delaware tribe chose him to record their part in the treaty of Easton, when the Indians agreed to make no settlements west of the Allegheny Mountains. Later they adopted Thomson into their tribe, giving him an Indian name meaning "man who tells the truth."

Thomson was active in opposing British tyranny before the Revolution and was a member of the famous Sons of Liberty group, which secretly worked against Britain. Joseph Galloway of Pennsylvania, who was such a bitter opponent of the struggle against Britain that he moved to England before the war was over, was Thomson's enemy and managed to prevent his being chosen as a delegate to the Continental Congress that carried on the war against Britain. He called Thomson "one of the most violent of the Sons of Liberty (so-called) in America."

But Thomson's good friend, John Adams, took a

different view of him. Adams's cousin, the patriot
Samuel Adams, was once called the "chief incendi-
ary" by royal Governor Thomas Hutchinson of Massachusetts because he never stopped fanning the
flame of revolution against Britain with his letters to
the newspapers and other activities. John Adams
called Charles Thomson "the Sam Adams of Philadelphia."

Thomson's failure to get into the Continental
Congress did not prevent him from serving it. In
spite of Galloway's opposition, he was chosen as its
secretary and remained so all through the Revolution. He became known as the "perpetual secretary"
because he continued in the post for so long.

Another honor awaited Thomson before he died.
When George Washington was elected the first President of the United States, Thomson was chosen to
notify him. Yet Washington does not seem to have
been one of his admirers. Thomson was given no
part in the inauguration ceremonies and despite his
abilities received no appointment in the new government of the United States. But these slights cannot overshadow the great service done for his country by this once indentured servant.

Daniel Dulaney was still another former indentured servant who made good. He also was an immigrant from Ireland but had a different background
from most who came from there. He was born into a
good family in Queens County (today it is County

Leix) in about 1685, was well educated and had some university training before he came to America with his two brothers when he was about eighteen.

They landed in Port Tobacco, Maryland, penniless. Ordinarily Daniel's education would have been of no value to an indentured servant and, like his brothers, he would have ended up as an indentured laborer in the tobacco fields. But a brighter future awaited him.

By chance a distinguished Maryland lawyer, a former attorney general of the province, was looking for just such a young man to do clerical work in his office and help with the accounts on the plantation he owned. He bought and indentured Daniel.

The lawyer was so impressed with Daniel's work that he aided him financially in studying law once his time of servitude was up. The former servant was admitted first to the bar in Charles County in 1709 and then to plead before the provincial court in 1710. But Daniel was not satisfied; in 1716 he went to London to study under the foremost lawyers of England at the famous Inns of Court.

Daniel Dulaney prospered when he returned to Maryland. He bought several thousand acres of land in western Maryland and encouraged German farmers from Pennsylvania to settle on his plantation.

He moved to Maryland's capital, Annapolis, in 1721 and was elected to the colony's assembly. In

1734 he became a judge of the admiralty court, hearing cases involving ships and shipping. He continued to serve in the assembly for twenty years and in 1742 became a member of the governor's council, where he remained eleven years until his death.

Other indentured servants rose high after their terms of servitude were completed. The story of the mighty soldier, Peter Francisco, has already been told. In Virginia, by 1654, several members of the colony's assembly were former servants, and in 1662 it was stated that most of the burgesses, members of the lower house of the Virginia Assembly, had been indentured. In Pennsylvania so many German settlers rose to political influence once they were free that other colonists feared they would completely dominate there and a law was passed forbidding German immigrants to vote, but this unfair limitation on their hard-won freedom was ended in 1731.

In South Carolina a number of artisans and mechanics rose to such prosperity after serving out their terms that they became members of the colony's aristocracy. Among them was a carpenter, Daniel Cannon, who made enough money to enable him to buy a plantation just outside Charleston. John Paul Grimké, a silversmith, had such success in selling his work that he came to own 500 acres on Edisto Island. Another silversmith, Jonathan Sarazin, bought 1,296 acres of land in St. John's Parish and went into the also profitable business of raising rice.

But for the immigration of an Irish couple to America, the colonists would not have had one noted Revolutionary general. John Sullivan of Limerick and Margery Browne of Cork came to Maine in 1723 as redemptioners. John Sullivan fell in love with Margery Browne, and since his term of indenture seems to have ended first, he is supposed to have bought her freedom and then married her. In 1740 their son John was born.

After serving as a major in the New Hampshire militia, the younger John Sullivan joined the Continental Army soon after the Revolution began and was shortly afterward made a brigadier general. He fought in the siege of Boston in 1775 and the invasion of Canada in 1775–76, was appointed major general during the campaign in New York, fought with distinction in the American victory over the Hessians at Trenton, New Jersey, the day after Christmas 1776, was in the battle of Brandywine and with Washington during the terrible winter at Valley Forge in 1777–78.

Sullivan's most famous exploit came in 1779, when he led an expedition into the country of the Six Nations, Indian allies of the British, in present-day New York State. He defeated the powerful Indian confederation, killed and captured many, laid waste to their villages and destroyed their usefulness to the British in the Revolution.

These are but a few of the success stories concerning indentured servants in America. Not all of them made good, but thousands did become fine, patriotic and prosperous citizens of the American colonies and later the new nation of the United States of America.

13

A SUMMING UP

In the seventeenth century, the system of indentured servitude arose out of the need for more workers in the American colonies and out of the desperate poverty in parts of Europe that made people willing to go somewhere, anywhere, to escape the intolerable conditions under which they lived. In some cases, as in Britain, governments encouraged the system, hoping to dispose of vast numbers of their countries' paupers, beggars, orphans, rogues and convicts.

Indentured servitude did help, to some extent, to rid Britain of her unwanted poor. It enabled thousands of English and Scottish and Irish people to find a better life, although not all survived to attain it. It gave a great number of Germans and German-speaking Swiss their chance for the same better life, and many succeeded admirably. It helped to fill the American colonies' need for labor. But there were too many bad aspects of the system.

Most of those who emigrated from Europe, whether by persuasion or their own choice, came with the idea that they would be well treated while they worked diligently to pay off their debts and that the eventual rewards would be great. Too many learned that neither assumption was true.

The indentured-servant system might have been better if only those who were decent but unfortunate had been allowed to emigrate under it from Britain and Ireland. In the case of the German-speaking emigrants, the overwhelming majority were good people, mostly farmers, along with artisans and mechanics, ready to work hard for a new start in life. Industrious and eager emigrants, wherever they came from, could all have become excellent, more or less prosperous citizens if they all had been given the proper chance. Some were, but others were not.

The spirits of England, the newlanders of Germany and other scurrilous characters who rounded up emigrants from Europe deliberately misled many into thinking life in America was a paradise with little hard work and no difficulties or hardships. Just as sailors were shanghaied aboard ships in the old days, these recruiters lured their prey with lies, picked up helpless drunkards and sometimes kidnaped those who could not resist, especially children.

If there had been decency for all in the way these servants were transported to America, another great evil would have been erased from the system. But the greed of merchants and shipowners in Europe and of the owners of indentured servants in America was responsible for too many voyages in which the emigrant passengers suffered the tortures of unbelievably cramped quarters, bad and scanty food, lack of ventilation and proper sanitary facilities, vermin, mistreatment and disease.

The usual method of selling servants and the practices of the soul-drivers were also a disgrace. Imported cattle received no worse treatment on their arrival at American seaports. And it was unfair and unproductive to put teachers, scholars and other cultured persons to work in tobacco and rice fields or to the exhausting labor of clearing forests and swamps. Either proper work for them should have been found or they should not have been allowed to come.

But by far the worst feature of the system was that indentured servitude was in fact a form of slavery, slavery as harsh and brutal in many cases as that experienced by blacks. Indentured servants had few of the rights of free citizens. They were owned by their masters, completely subject to their wishes and desires, for a period of years that could be much longer than anticipated. Some masters treated their servants decently, but too many housed and fed them poorly, beat them for small offenses and even murdered them.

Freedom is the very keynote of the United States of America today, and during the Revolution colonists risked their lives to gain it. Yet they saw nothing wrong in enslaving other human beings, white as well as black, to satisfy their own needs.

The white slaves of the seventeenth and eighteenth centuries have been almost forgotten today. Yet without these "colonists for sale" the settlement and development of a country that was to become the richest and most powerful free nation on earth would have been seriously hampered. Nevertheless, the injustices and brutalities of the system under which the indentured servants lived remain a shameful chapter in the history of the United States.

FOR FURTHER READING

Unfortunately, few of the books and publications used as research sources in this book are easily obtainable in any but the largest libraries with well-established reference departments. Those who live in the states whose historical society publications and journals are listed in the bibliography can more easily obtain them for full reading on the subjects.

For books which may be in the collections of smaller libraries, Abbott Emerson Smith's *Colonists in Bondage* is easily the best and most complete book on white indentured servitude in the American colonies. Richard Hofstadter, in *America at 1750*, has an excellent chapter on white servitude, as well as chapters on the black slave trade and slavery and a first-class picture of what America was like in the middle of the eighteenth century.

Mark Boatner III's *Encyclopedia of the American Revolution*, one of the best Revolutionary history sources in existence, tells of Peter Francisco's military service in detail.

For background on the causes of Irish emigration to America, Seumas MacManus's *The Story of the Irish Race* is a long but entertaining volume that should be found on the shelves of most good-sized libraries. It tells the full story of Ireland's persecution and suffering over the centuries.

BIBLIOGRAPHY

Adams, Charles Francis. *Three Episodes of Massachusetts History*. Boston: Houghton Mifflin, 1892.

Alderman, Clifford Lindsey. *The Story of the Thirteen Colonies*. New York: Random, 1966.

Ballagh, James Curtis. *White Servitude in the Colony of Virginia*. Baltimore: Johns Hopkins Press, 1895.

Besant, Walter. *London in the Days of the Stuarts*. London: Adam & Charles Black, 1903.

Blake, John W. "Transportation from Ireland to America, 1653–1660." *Irish Historical Studies*, 3, no. 11 (March 1943).

Boatner, Mark Mayo III. *Encylopedia of the American Revolution*. New York: McKay, 1966.

Buettner, Johann Carl. *Narrative of Johann Carl Buettner in the American Revolution*. New York: Charles Frederick Heartman, 1915.

Burke, Thomas. *The Streets of London*. London: B. T. Batsford, 1940.

Bushnell, George Eleazer. *Bushnell Family Genealogy*. Nashville: Compiled by the author, 1945.

Coleman, R. V. *The First Frontier*. New York: Scribner, 1948.

BIBLIOGRAPHY

Crane, Charles Edward. *Let Me Show You Vermont.* New York: Knopf, 1946.

Craven, Wesley Frank. *The Southern Colonies in the Seventeenth Century.* Baton Rouge: Louisiana State University Press, 1940.

Dobson, Meade C. "The True Story of Captain Kidd." *Nassau County Historical Society Journal,* 13, no. 2 (Spring 1962).

Earle, Alice Morse. *Home Life in Colonial Days.* New York: Grosset & Dunlap, 1898.

Eddis, William. *Letters from America.* Cambridge: Harvard University Press, 1969.

Ellis, Edward Robb. *The Epic of New York City.* New York: Coward McCann, 1966.

Erlich, Blake. *London on the Thames.* Boston: Little, Brown, 1966.

Fox, Loyal Stephen. "Colonel Matthew Lyon—Biographical and Genealogical Notes." *Vermont Quarterly,* n.s. 12, no. 3 (July 1944).

Geiser, Frederick. *Redemptioners and Indentured Servants in the Colony and Commonwealth of Pennsylvania.* New Haven: Tuttle, Morchouse & Taylor, 1901.

Gipson, Henry Lawrence. *The British Isles and the American Colonies.* New York: Knopf, 1958.

Henderson, Ernest F. *A Short History of Germany.* New York: Macmillan, 1917.

Herrick, Cheesman A. *White Servitude in Pennsylvania.* Philadelphia: John Joseph McVey, 1926.

Hibbert, Christopher. *London, the Biography of a City.* New York: Morrow, 1969.

Hofstadter, Richard. *America at 1750.* New York: Knopf, 1971.

Knittle, Walter Allen. *Early Eighteenth Century Palatine Emigration.* Philadelphia: Dorrance & Co., 1937.

MacManus, Seumas. *The Story of the Irish Race.* New York: Devin-Adair, 1970.

McCormac, Eugene Irving. "White Servitude in Maryland, 1634–1820." *Johns Hopkins New Studies in Historical and Political Science*, 22d ser., no. 3, no. 4 (1904).

McKee, Samuel, Jr. "Indentured Servitude in Colonial New York." *New York State Historical Association Quarterly Journal*, vol. 12 (1931).

Miller, William. "The Effects of the American Revolution on Industrial Servitude." *Pennsylvania History*, 7, no. 3 (July 1940).

Mitchell, R. J. and Leys, M. D. R. *A History of London Life*. London: Longmans, Green, 1958.

Mittelberger, Gottfried. *Gottfried Mittelberger's Journey to Pennsylvania in the Year 1750 and Return to Germany*. Philadelphia: John Joseph McVey, 1898.

Newton, Earle. *The Vermont Story*. Montpelier: Vermont Historical Society, 1949.

Ogg, David. *England in the Reign of Charles II*. Oxford: Clarendon Press, 1934.

Porter, Nannie Francisco, and Albertson, Catherine Fauntleroy. *The Romantic Record of Peter Francisco*. Staunton, Va.: McClure Co., 1929.

Quennell, Marjorie, and Quennell, C. H. B. *A History of Everyday Things in England*. London: B. T. Batsford, 1950.

Rees, Goronwy. *The Rhine*. New York: Putnam, 1967.

Saybrook Tercentenary Committee. *In the Land of the Patentees, Saybrook in Connecticut*. Saybrook: Acton Library, 1935.

Semmes, Ralph. *Crime and Punishment in Early Maryland*. Baltimore: Johns Hopkins Press, 1938.

Sister Margaret Patricia. "White Servitude in the American Colonies." American Catholic Historical Society of Philadelphia. Records. Vol. 49, no. 1 (March 1931).

Smith, Abbott Emerson. *Colonists in Bondage*. Chapel Hill: University of North Carolina Press, 1947.

―――. "Indentured Servants. New Light on America's 'First' Families." *Journal of Economic History*, 2, no. 1 (May 1942).

Smith, Goldwyn. *A History of England*. New York: Scribner, 1966.

Smith, Warren B. *White Servitude in Colonial South Carolina*. Columbia: University of South Carolina Press, 1901.

Stuart, William. "White Servitude in New York and New Jersey." *Americana* (American Historical Magazine), 15 (January 1921–December 1921).

Treharne, R. E., and Fullard, Harold, eds. *Muir's New School Atlas of Universal History*. New York: Barnes & Noble, 1961.

Van Doren, Carl. *Benjamin Franklin*. New York: Viking, 1938.

Wade, Herbert Treadwell. *A Brief History of the Colonial Wars in America*. New York: Society of Colonial Wars in the State of New York, 1948.

Warwick, Edward; Ritz, Henry C.; Wyckoff, Alexander. *Early American Dress*. New York: Benjamin Blom, 1965.

Willison, George F. *Saints and Strangers, the Story of the Mayflower and the Plymouth Colony*. London: Heinemann, 1966.

Winsor, Justin, ed. *The Memorial History of Boston*. Boston: James R. Osgood, 1881.

Wish, Harvey. *Society and Thought in Early America*. New York: Longmans, Green, 1950.

Wolf, John B. *Louis XIV*. New York: Norton, 1968.

Woodward, G. W. O. *The Dissolution of the Monasteries*. New York: Walker, 1967.

(No author) *Biographical Directory of the American Congress, 1774–1961*. Washington: Government Printing Office, 1961.

(No author) "Peter Francisco, the American Soldier." *William & Mary Quarterly*, 13, no. 4 (April 1905).

INDEX

Acadians, 87, 88, 99, 100
Agents, 30, 42, 43, 45, 49, 74
Annersley, James, 46–48
Apleonya, Anna, 104, 105
Apprentices, 12, 34, 76, 77
Argall, Gov. Samuel, 55

Bacon, Jabez, 159
Baltimore, Lord, *see* Calvert
Benefits, servants', 50, 62, 63, 64
Berkeley Hundred, Va., 23, 24
Black servants, 62
Bradnox, Capt. Thomas, 69–71
Broadsides, 22, 23, 25–28
Brown, Joshua, 49
Buettner, Johann Karl, 39, 40, 144, 145
Bushnell, Joshua, Jr., 138, 139

Calvert, James, Lord Baltimore, 72
Catholics, dislike of, 20, 42, 43, 48, 72, 133, 134
Charles II, 14, 59, 91
Charles City Hundred, 56
Church of England, 13, 72, 127
Church of Rome, 13
Colonial wars, 121, 140–144, 157

Continental Congress, 157, 158, 159
Convicts, 59, 88, 99, 108
Cooks' houses, 33, 34
Cromwell, Oliver, 20, 43, 59, 72, 91
"Custom of the country," 57–58

Dale, Sir Thomas, 54, 55
Dandy, James, 71
Daser, 81–82
Declaration of Independence, 158–159
Delaware, servants in, 90
Delaware, Lord Thomas, 53–54
Diseases among servants, 54–55
Dudley, Thomas, 128
Dulaney, Daniel, 167–169
Dutch Church of New York, 118–119

Eddis, William, 69
Ellis, Robert, 47
Emigrants, Barbados, 94
Emigrants, Dutch, 106, 107
Emigrants, English, 17, 22–24, 30–36, 94, 172
Emigrants, German, 2–8, 20, 26, 36–41, 109–122, 172
Emigrants, Irish, 22, 27, 42–45, 48, 52, 172

Emigrants, Scottish, 21, 22, 26–27, 48, 49–52, 172

Emigrants, Swiss, 26, 27, 37–38, 41, 172

England, conditions in, 13–17, 28–30

English Rogue, the, 34–35

Enlistment, servants, 140–145, 146

Fincher, Joseph, 71

Fitcher, 129–130

Francisco, Peter, 146–152

Franklin, Benjamin, 76, 153

Free-willers, 107, 108, 110

Freedom dues, 57–58, 65, 74–75, 88, 89, 101, 104, 110, 111, 124, 125–126, 134–136

Georgia, servants in, 105–106

German Society of Philadelphia, 85

Germany, conditions in, 18–20

Gerrard, Thomas, 73

Gouge, Henry, 71

Grimké, Paul, 169

Haggmann, Jeffery, 71

Hanley, Elizabeth, 137–139

Hocking, Capt., 155, 156

Howe, Millicent, 93

Howland, John, 154–156

Hunter, Gov. Robert, 114, 115–116, 117–118, 120–121

Hunting, John, 135

Indentures, 8–10, 23, 36, 45, 50, 57, 62, 63, 67, 73, 74, 93, 94, 96, 124

Indian wars, 97, 98

Indians, 11, 118, 130–131

Inducements to settlers, 23

Ireland, conditions in, 20–21, 42–44

James I, 22, 130

James II, 59–60, 99

Jamestown, Va., 11, 22

Kidd, Capt. William, 122, 123

Kidnaping, 33, 36, 46, 49–52, 72

Le Brasseur, Francis, 104

Lewger, John, 75

Life of servants, 60–64, 65, 67, 68, 69, 79–82, 83, 84, 85, 89, 90, 112–115, 118–120, 122, 123, 126, 129–139, 174, 175

Littlefield, Abigail, 135

Livingston Manor, 113, 114, 120

Livingston, Robert, 113, 114

London, 17, 22, 28–30, 31, 32, 34, 35, 44, 59, 78, 102, 105, 109, 111, 120

Lyon, Matthew, 159–165

Marki, Jacob, 104

Maryland, servants in, 66–77, 142